# THE COMPLETE BOOK OF
# Nature Craft
# Techniques

# The Complete Book of
# Nature Craft
# Techniques

From Baskets and Bows
to Vinegars and Wreaths,
Everything You Need to Know
to Craft with Natural Materials

Deborah Morgenthal
and Chris Rich

Rodale Press, Inc.
Emmaus, Pennsylvania

## OUR MISSION

*We publish books that empower people's lives.*

RODALE BOOKS

Published in 1996 by Rodale Press, Inc.

Rodale Press Staff:
>    Vice President and Editorial Director, Home and Garden: Margaret Lydic Balitas
>    Editors: Marya Kissinger Amig and Cheryl Winters Tetreau
>    Interior Book Designer: Patricia Field
>    Horticultural Consultants: Nancy J. Ondra and Heidi Stonehill
>    Cover Designer: Catherine Mace
>    Front Cover Photographer: John Hamel
>    Cover Photo Stylist: Marianne Grape Laubach
>    Copy Editor: Maria Kasprenski Zator
>    Manufacturing Coordinator: Jodi Schaffer

Created and Produced by Altamont Press, Inc.
50 College Street, Asheville, NC 28801

Altamont Press Staff:
>    Art/Production: Elaine Thompson and Chris Colando
>    Back Cover Photographer: Evan Bracken

The editors who compiled this book have tried to make all of the contents as accurate and as correct as possible. Illustrations, photographs, and text have all been carefully checked and cross-checked. However, due to the variability of materials, personal skill, and so on, neither the editors nor Rodale Press assumes any responsibility for any injuries suffered or for damages or other losses incurred that result from the material presented herein. All instructions should be carefully studied and clearly understood before beginning a project.

The editors at Rodale Press hope you will join with us in preserving nature's beauty so that others may share in the enjoyment of nature crafting. Unless you are certain that the plants or plant materials you are collecting—including leaves, stems, bark, flowers, fruits, seeds, or roots—are very common in your area, or over a wide geographic area, please do not collect them. Do not disturb or collect any plants or plant materials from parks, natural areas, or private lands without the permission of the owner.

> To the best of our knowledge, the plants and plant materials recommended in this book are common natural materials that can be grown and collected without harm to the environment.

*On the cover (clockwise from bottom left):* Engraved Autumnal Gourds (page 143), Root & Flower Wreath (page 234), Bark Baskets (page 11), Iris & Willow Potato Basket (page 35), Twig Basket (page 223)

If you have any questions or comments concerning this book, please write to:
>    Rodale Press, Inc.
>    Book Readers' Service
>    33 East Minor Street
>    Emmaus, PA 18098

**Library of Congress Cataloging-in-Publication Data**
Morgenthal, Deborah, date
      The complete book of nature craft techniques : from baskets and bows to vinegars and wreaths, everything you need to know to craft with natural materials / by Deborah Morgenthal and Chris Rich.
            p.    cm.
      Includes bibliographical references and index.
      ISBN 0–87596–714–0 (alk. paper) hardcover
      1. Nature craft.    I. Rich, Chris, 1949–    .   II. Title.
TT157.M635    1996
745.5--dc20                                                                    95–26291
                                                                                      CIP

ISBN 0-87596-714-0 hardcover

Printed in the United States of America on acid-free ∞ , recycled ♻ paper

**Distributed in the book trade by St. Martin's Press**

2  4  6  8  10  9  7  5  3  1    hardcover

# CONTENTS

# INTRODUCTION

In nature crafts, as in many aspects of life, there are two types of people. The first type sees a beautiful wreath, basket, or carved gourd in a craft store and exclaims, "I could make this!" The second type sees the same item and regretfully sighs, "I could never make this." Do you recognize which type you are?

The mission of this book is twofold: To inspire the crafters in the first group by providing them with a wealth of information and a lot of enticing projects so that they can live up to their own expectations, and to convince the folks in the second group that with the right tools, techniques, and materials, they most certainly can learn to make a whole variety of nature crafts.

No matter which type you are, we believe that this book, written in an A to Z format, will answer all your questions about nature-craft techniques. It's all here: drying flowers, making wreath bases, weaving wheat, tying bows, collecting natural materials—one glance at the "Contents" on page 5 will show you how comprehensive the book is. Each major category of natural material is explored so that you'll have an even greater appreciation of Mother Nature's amazing gifts. You'll learn how to handle a hot-glue gun and when and why to use floral pins, picks, and tape. Plus you can practice these techniques by making more than 80 eye-catching projects, including bark baskets, cornhusk dolls, dried flower wreaths, handmade paper, potpourris, terrariums, vinegars, and much, much more.

*The Complete Book of Nature Craft Techniques,* brimming with hints, tips, and projects, has something for everyone interested in this popular activity, from the beginner to the expert. If you're skilled at wreathmaking, here's your opportunity to learn how to make paper or paint a gourd. If you've never so much as pressed a flower, here's your chance to learn how.

Skim through the book for a minute: See that gorgeous swag on page 204? You can make it. Oh, and that stunning pine-needle basket on page 184—you can make that, too. Why are you waiting? Let's get started.

## How to Use This Book

The book is organized alphabetically into 37 sections that represent the major nature-craft techniques, tools, and supplies, as well as the most commonly used materials. Step-by-step instructions and color photographs demonstrate how to clean and prepare a cured gourd, how to make a straw base, two types of bows, a cornhusk doll, a flower arrangement, handmade papers, a terrarium, tussie mussies, a twig basket, and an evergreen wreath. There are detailed instructions, often accompanied by illustrations, for making dozens and dozens of projects that use the various techniques and materials discussed.

There are a few ways that you can use this book. You can start with "Apples" and work your way through the alphabet to "Zinnias"—a great option if you have unlimited time! It's more likely that you'll begin with a technique that interests you. For instance, let's say you want to learn how to make a wreath. You might begin by turning to "Wreaths" and reading the entire chapter. In the process, you'll be referred to "Bases" for information on how to make your own base. (There are a number of cross-references like this throughout the book.) You'll also be referred to the different types of materials often used in wreaths, such as berries, pods, and herbs. You may want to look at those chapters to see what your options are. Returning to the wreath chapter, you may decide to take advantage of the how-to project that will take you through all the steps for making an evergreen wreath.

Another approach would be to use the index and start by looking up the material you want to use in your wreath—dried flowers, for example. You would turn to the chapter on "Drying," where a great deal of information is given on different kinds of dried flowers, along with several dried flower wreath projects. Then you could jump right in by making the wreath that most appeals to you. Or, you could turn to the index where you'll find a listing for "Wreaths" with all the wreath projects in the book identified in one place.

Each project in the book features a comprehensive list of materials, tools, and supplies, with the natural materials mentioned first and in the order in which you will use them; the other materials, tools, and supplies are then listed, again in order of use. Exact amounts and sizes of each type of material are given. Feel free to substitute other materials that you prefer or that are more available to you. Alter sizes and quantities, too. And by all means—if you would rather wire the flower on, instead of hot-gluing it—go right ahead. We do not intend for the lists, materials, and instructions to stifle you, but rather, to make certain that if you choose to follow them as they are written, you will wind up with a project that closely resembles the one in the photograph.

If you are planning to collect your own wild materials, please be sure you know which plant species are endangered and avoid harvesting them. Also, try not to collect too many materials of any kind from one locale. And please be considerate and always ask permission before harvesting on private property.

There are many ways to describe one or more flowers or plants. To be consistent and clear, we devised the following working definitions:

**Bloom** Single, simple flower without a stem, such as a marigold bloom.

**Bunch** A large amount of one material as sold by florists, craft-supply stores, and mail-order catalogues.

**Bundle or cluster** Three to seven stems of one or more flowers or herbs.

**Flower head** Complex blooms of a flower or herb, with the stem cut off, such as a yarrow flower head.

**Sprig** One of or a piece of the smaller branching stems taken from a larger stem, such as baby's-breath, juniper, sweet Annie, statice, and artemisia.

**Stem** Complete plant material with or without the flowering part, such as a stem of oregano or a stem of hydrangea.

There are many excellent books on the market that offer detailed instructions on a single nature craft, such as basketry or flower arranging. If a topic in this book whets your appetite and makes you eager to learn more, we encourage you to do so.

In whatever way you choose to use this book, it is our sincere hope that it will open the door to the rewarding world of making beautiful crafts, thanks to nature's bounty and your own capable hands. Happy crafting!

# A APPLES

Apples are plentiful, inexpensive, delightfully fragrant, and available throughout the year. What's more, they're easy to incorporate into craft designs.

If you've never used apples as craft material, you're in for a surprise. Whole, fresh, red apples add a special touch to seasonal wreaths. To help apples retain their shiny appearance and solid shape, dip them into acrylic floor wax and let the wax dry thoroughly before using them in your project.

Dried, chopped apples add a delicious tang to teas, as well as fragrance and texture to potpourri. When designing fragrant projects, keep in mind that apples work well with the spices that accompany them in cooking: cloves, cinnamon, and nutmeg.

Dried apple slices are perfect for nature crafts, as you'll discover when you make this decorative garland.

# Kitchen Garland

## WHAT YOU NEED

4 garlic bulbs

5 dried pomegranates

320 whole bay leaves

30 dried apple slices

Electric drill with $\frac{1}{32}$-inch drill bit

44 inches of plastic-coated floral wire

Wire cutters

Masking tape

Several lengths of raffia

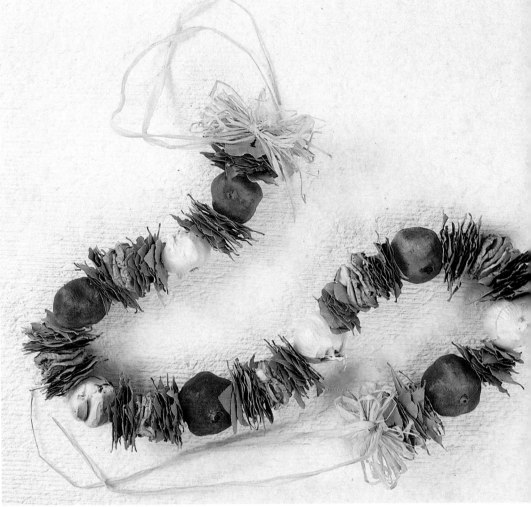

## WHAT YOU DO

*1* If you want to dry your own pomegranates, follow the instructions on page 84 in the "Drying" section. Then, using the drill and bit, bore holes through the centers of the garlic bulbs and the dried pomegranates.

*2* Using the wire cutters, cut one end of the wire at an angle to create a sharp point. Mark the center of the wire with a small piece of masking tape. Thread one pomegranate onto the sharpened wire, centering it over the masking tape. Continue threading the materials onto the sharpened wire in the following order: 20 bay leaves, 5 apple slices, 20 bay leaves, 1 garlic bulb, 20 bay leaves, 5 apple slices, 20 bay leaves, 1 pomegranate, 20 bay leaves, 5 apple slices, 20 bay leaves, 1 garlic bulb, 20 bay leaves, 1 pomegranate, and 20 bay leaves.

When all the materials are strung, blunt-cut the wire.

*3* Cut the other end of the wire at an angle to create a sharp point. Thread the rest of the materials onto the sharpened wire in the same order listed in Step 2, starting with the 20 bay leaves. When all the materials are strung, blunt-cut the wire.

*4* Twist each end of the wire to form a secure loop and trim the ends as necessary. Make a raffia bow and tie it just below each wire loop.

*5* Using one loop or both, suspend the garland on a wall, over a cabinet door, or around a window or doorway.

*For another project with apples, see page 188.*

*Designed to grace a wall or cabinet, this colorful strand of culinary materials will lift your spirits every time you walk into the kitchen.*

# B  BARK

Today, we barely notice bark until it's brought to our attention, but our ancestors knew a good thing when they saw it. For centuries, this flexible and resilient material has been gathered and shaped to make functional and decorative items.

Harvesting tree bark isn't difficult, but you need to know what you're doing before you start. Bark textures vary from species to species. To make the basket presented in this chapter, select trees with bark that is relatively smooth and flexible. Birches, yellow poplars, young maples, aspens, and cottonwoods are all suitable.

Although it's possible to strip bark from old logs, bark removed from green logs is much more supple, especially if you use it within a couple days of harvesting it. Fell your tree during the spring or summer; after the first frost, the bark won't peel properly from green logs.

To preserve the global tree population, exercise restraint when selecting trees. Unless you're working in your own well-managed woodlot, choose only saplings that need to come down. Remove all the usable bark and make more than one project. For example, you can use the stripped logs for fence posts or firewood. Take special care when working with the sharp tools used to harvest tree bark.

To make the attractive wallhanging in this chapter, you'll need a three-dimensional piece of "found" bark that has fallen from a tree. Set aside a sunny day for a bark-seeking stroll along your favorite woodland path. Your "found" bark won't match the birch bark in this project exactly, so adapt the project instructions as needed.

## Harvesting Bark for Baskets

Start with a young, second-growth tree, no larger than 10 inches in diameter. Fell the tree using a handsaw or axe. Using the same tool, remove all the branches as close to the trunk as possible. Cut the trunk into 6-foot-long sections.

Using a linoleum (or hawk-billed) knife, split the outer bark down the entire length of the log. Insert a chisel or spud into the split and gradually pry the bark from the log, alternating sides as you work. (A spud—a green stick, ½ inch in diameter, which is cut at one end to resemble a chisel blade—is less likely to scar the inner surface of the bark.) Continue until the bark pops off the log.

# Bark Baskets

*These rustic baskets make eye-catching containers for anything from dried flowers from your garden to after-school snacks for your children.*

## WHAT YOU NEED (for 1 basket)

Harvested bark

Linoleum knife or hawk-billed knife

Tape measure

Pencil

Straightedge

Large rubber band

Electric drill and ¹⁄₁₆-inch drill bit,
   or a hammer and awl

48 inches of jute twine

Curved upholstery needle with large eye

Scissors

Several sheets of newspaper (optional)

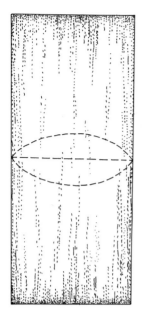

*Figure 1*

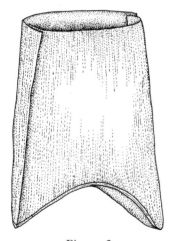

*Figure 2*

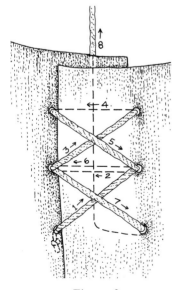

*Figure 3*

## WHAT YOU DO

*1* While the harvested bark is still wet and pliable, use the knife to cut the bark into 12 × 24-inch rectangles.

*2* Position one bark rectangle on a flat work surface, with its outer surface facing up. Use the tape measure and the pencil to measure and mark the center point along each long edge. Then, using the straightedge and the pencil, draw a straight line to join the two points. On each side of the center line, draw an arc (see Figure 1). The two arcs should form a carefully proportioned "cat's eye."

*3* Use the knife to score both arcs lightly, piercing only the outermost bark layer. Make sure that the cuts meet precisely at each edge of the bark.

*4* Lift up the bark rectangle and carefully fold it along the scored lines to form a basket with an eye-shaped bottom. The long edges of the bark should overlap on both sides of the basket (see Figure 2).

*5* Place a large rubber band around the basket to secure it.

*6* To fasten the sides of the basket, you'll lace them up as if you were lacing a shoe, but you'll use only one piece of jute twine. (Lacing patterns can vary, but beginners should start with the one described here.) Using the pattern shown in Figure 3, mark six holes on each side of the basket, starting about ½ inch from the top.

*7* Bore the marked holes with the drill bit or the awl, making the holes large enough to accommodate the twine.

*8* Tie a large knot at one end of the twine and thread the other end through the upholstery needle.

*9* Following the numbered sequence shown in Figure 3, start lacing the twine from the bottom inside surface of the basket, continuing up the outer surface and back down again. The twine will end up coming out on the inside at the bottom. Thread this end of the twine up underneath the center of the lacing on the inside of the basket. When you reach the top set of holes, tie another tight knot on the inside surface to prevent the sides of the basket from pulling apart. Leaving about 12 to 18 inches of twine to serve as a handle, bring the twine down and start lacing again from an inside bottom hole on the opposite side of the basket. Repeat the lacing process on this side and tie a secure knot when you're finished. With the scissors, trim the ends of the twine as necessary.

*10* Remove the rubber band from the basket and hang the basket by its twine handle to dry. This will take about three weeks. Don't worry if you notice an unattractive odor during this time; bark smells less than appealing as it dries, but the odor will disappear. In extremely dry areas, the edges may curl as the basket cures. To prevent this from happening, stuff the basket tightly with crumpled newspaper, if desired.

# Woodland Bark Curl

*You can find nature's bounties everywhere. This piece of "found" bark has been transformed into a decorative wallhanging.*

## WHAT YOU NEED

1 piece of three-dimensional "found" bark

16 dried magnolia leaves

5 assorted feathers, 5 inches long

3 or 4 stems of dried statice, 12 to 15 inches long

12 stems of dried astilbe, 12 inches long

4 love-in-a-mist seed heads

1 piece of heavy-duty cardboard, at least 6 inches square

Scissors or sharp knife

Wire cutters

Spool of medium-gauge floral wire

1 piece of felt, 10 inches square

Hot-glue gun and glue sticks

Wood glue

Heavy object, like a rock

Sahara foam

6 craft picks

Red spray paint

1 artificial bird

Spray shellac

## WHAT YOU DO

*1* To make a wall-mounting plate for this project, use the scissors or the knife to cut a piece of cardboard just large enough to help stabilize the curl against the wall, but not so large that the plate will show once it has been glued to the back of the project.

*2* To make a hanger for the cardboard plate, use the point of the scissors or the knife to poke two small holes through the center of the cardboard, spacing them about 3 inches apart. Using the wire cutters, cut a 7-inch-long piece of the floral wire. Insert one end of the wire into one hole and form that end into a coil to prevent it from slipping back through the hole. Repeat with the other end of the wire and the other hole, leaving enough wire between the holes to serve as a hanger.

*3* Cut a slit in the felt piece, locating it in approximately the same position on the felt as the wire hanger occupies on the mounting plate. Place the felt over the plate, slipping the wire through the slit. Bring the edges of the felt around to the back of the plate, hot-gluing the felt to the cardboard wherever necessary. Trim away any excess felt.

*4* Brush away any debris from the inner portions of the bark curl. Center the bark curl on the back of the plate. Remove the curl, spread a small pool of wood glue on the plate, and replace the curl. Press the bark against the plate by inserting a heavy object, such as a rock, into the curl. Set the project aside to dry for 24 hours.

*5* Using the photo on page 13 as a guide, hot-glue ten of the magnolia leaves between the mounting plate and the curl, five above and five below the center point. Note that these leaves should disguise any visible portions of the plate.

*6* Fill both ends of the bark curl with Sahara foam, adding wedges of foam until the foam is secure.

*7* If the remaining six magnolia leaves lack stems, hot-glue them to craft picks. At each end of the bark curl, insert three magnolia leaves and the feathers into the Sahara foam toward the back of the curl. Break small sections of the statice from the long stems and insert them to form a feathery cloud in front of the leaves and the feathers.

*8* Break off and discard a few inches of each stem of astilbe, leaving 2 to 3 inches of stem on each piece. Spray paint the astilbe red and allow it to dry.

*9* Insert the painted astilbe stems into the foam at each end of the bark curl so that only the blooms show, locating them toward the front of the project to create a layered effect. Then insert the love-in-a-mist seed heads toward the front at each end. Hot-glue the bird in place on the outside of the curl.

*10* To preserve the project's colors, carefully spray it with shellac.

# BASES

When you plan to make a wreath, swag, or garland, your first decision will be what type of base to use. A base provides the support for the natural materials and other items that are attached to it. When you make a wreath, for example, the kind of base you need will be determined by the kinds of materials you plan to use to create your wreath and the overall look you want to achieve. Larger materials demand a larger base in order to look well proportioned. Heavier items must be secured so they won't fall off and to prevent the wreath from sagging. The most commonly used bases are vine, straw, and wire, followed by moss-covered, twig, and polystyrene.

The role that the base will play and the types of decorative elements that will be attached will help you decide what kind of base you need. If you plan to attach dozens of small clusters of dried flowers using floral picks, a straw or polystyrene base will work well. But if you plan to cover the entire base by gluing on heavy shells, you might favor a straw base reinforced with wire. If you don't want to cover the entire base with materials, you'll want a base that looks attractive when unadorned, such as grapevine or moss-covered. "Wreath Base Options" on page 21 highlights the main advantages, drawbacks, and attachment methods for each type of base.

Craft-supply stores and many discount outlets carry reasonably priced wreath bases in many different sizes and made from a remarkable variety of natural materials, including eucalyptus stems, juniper branches, rye stems, and magnolia leaves. But it is easy and rewarding to make your own base. Simply follow the instructions in this chapter to make straw, vine, twig, and moss-covered bases.

## Straw Bases

Straw bases are easy to make. Any type of hay, alfalfa, or dried grasses can be fashioned into a base of the size and shape you want. Straw bases are usually completely covered with materials to "hide" their appearance. But because it's easy to attach materials to these bases with floral picks, wire, or hot glue, these ugly ducklings are a favorite among wreath designers. Straw bases are especially reliable if you'll be attaching heavy items, such as whole, dried fruit.

To make a strong straw base, it's good to aim for a thickness of 2 to 3 inches, but a thinner or thicker base may be more appropriate for your wreath design. You may want to wear cloth gardening gloves to protect your hands from the straw's slivers and sharp ends.

# Straw Base

## WHAT YOU NEED

6 to 12 large handfuls of straw

1 wire coat hanger or 39½ inches of heavy-gauge wire

Wire cutters

Needle-nose pliers

Spool of fine-gauge floral wire

## WHAT YOU DO

*1* Unbend the coat hanger or the heavy-gauge wire and shape it into a circle that is about 12 inches in diameter. Use the needle-nose pliers to twist the two wire ends together.

*2* Start with a large handful of straw, compress it tightly, and position it against the wire ring. (If you're right-handed, hold the straw and the wire circle in your left hand.)

*3* With your other hand, wind the floral wire two or three times around the straw and the wire circle in 1½- to 2-inch intervals. Make sure the wire is tight enough to bundle the straw securely. Loop the starting end of the wire around a section of the wrapped wire to hold it in place.

4 Continue adding handfuls of straw of the same thickness and securing the straw with floral wire. Each new handful should slightly overlap the preceding one. Keep unwinding the wire from the spool; don't cut it until you have the entire base covered with straw.

5 Finish assembling the base by wrapping the floral wire three times around the straw in the same place and trimming it with the wire cutters. For a thicker wreath, wire on another layer of straw. The base can now be shaped into a more precise circle, if desired, or reshaped into an oval or a square.

## Vine and Twig Bases

Vine and twig bases are popular because their natural beauty allows the designer to leave portions of the base exposed. In fact, the base becomes an important design element of the floral arrangement. Craft-supply stores carry a wide range of vine and twig bases, such as grapevine hearts, ovals, bows, and circles; huckleberry wreaths and arches; and trellis forms made from twigs. You can often find many of these bases at florist shops, and a smaller selection is usually available at discount outlets.

Why not try to collect your own vines and twigs and make your own base? It's easy and fun. Grapevine is the sturdiest; honeysuckle and wisteria are nearly as strong but have a more delicate appearance. Bittersweet, huckleberry, and catbrier can also be fashioned into distinctive-looking bases. Kudzu, the fast-growing Asian vine (and the bane of gardeners in the Southeast!), makes a very sturdy base, too (see "Wild Wreath" on page 235). Birch, dogwood, elm,

fantail pussy willow, hemlock, silver maple, sycamore, and willow are sources of good-quality twigs. Pine isn't a good choice because it oozes sap for quite a while after it's been cut. For a discussion of how to collect and handle cut vines and twigs, see "Vines" on page 231 and "Twigs" on page 221.

To form bases for short swags, wire several vines or twigs together at the center, using medium- or heavy-gauge floral wire (see Figure 1). Vine and twig wreath bases are just as easy to make as you will see from the following two sets of instructions.

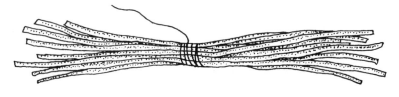

*Figure 1*

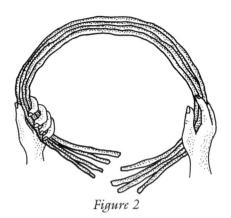

*Figure 2*

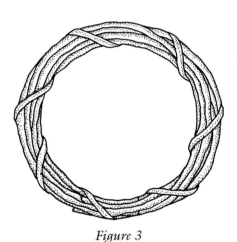

*Figure 3*

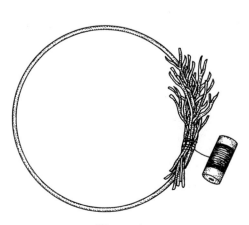

*Figure 4*

## Making a Vine Wreath Base

If you are working with short lengths of vine, hold six to eight lengths (15 inches or less) together and bend them to form a circle a little larger than you want your finished wreath to be (see Figure 2). Leave a 2-inch overlap at the ends and secure the lengths of vine together by wrapping a single 6-inch-long vine horizontally over the overlapped ends.

If you're working with a very long vine (3 to 4 feet long), form a circle the size you want the wreath to be and continue winding the long vine around this circle until the base is as thick as you want it. Secure the rounds by wrapping the vine horizontally around the base (see Figure 3).

Much of the charm of a vine base is the material itself: The meandering tendrils add excitement and a sense of movement. Experiment with the base by wrapping the circle shape with more vines or winding all of them either in one direction or in alternating directions. If you want a different look, you can spray your finished base a color that matches your decor.

## Making a Twig Base

Unbend a wire coat hanger and shape it into a circle, twisting the ends to secure them.

Assemble 16 bunches of twigs (4 to 5 inches long), each with five twigs. Fasten each bunch with a rubber band at one end.

Attach the bunches to the wire circle with floral wire, overlapping each bunch to hide the rubber band (see Figure 4). Do not cut the wire; keep wrapping until the entire circle is covered with the twig clusters.

When you are finished assembling the base, wrap the wire around the twig clusters and the wire circle at least three times and then cut the wire. You can try this technique with pussy willows, too. Cut the willow stems to 4-inch lengths and wire them individually to a wire base.

## Moss-Covered Bases

Moss is a wonderful medium for a base, and you can use a variety of mosses. Depending on the kind you use, you can create a base that is rustic, delicate, unobtrusive, neutral, or dramatic. Another attraction of moss is that plant material can be easily picked or hot-glued onto the moss (see "Mosses, Lichens, & Fungi" on page 168). Moss-covered bases in a range of sizes are available commercially, but you can easily make them yourself in just the right size and shape for your project. For tips on gathering fresh moss, see "Harvesting Moss" on page 168.

To cover a polystyrene or a straw base with Spanish moss, simply arrange the moss around the top and sides of the base and then secure it in place with floral pins or with loose wraps of monofilament or medium-gauge floral wire (see Figure 5). If you are using sheet or mood moss, simply wrap it around the base and secure it with floral pins. It's best to try this when the moss is still damp so that it won't break when you curve it around the polystyrene or straw base.

To make a Spanish-moss base from scratch, you will need several large handfuls of moss, an unbent coat hanger or a 24- to 36-inch length of heavy-gauge wire, and a spool of monofilament or medium-gauge wire. First, shape the coat hanger or the heavy-gauge wire into a circle slightly smaller than the size you want the wreath base to be. Similar to the instructions for making a straw base (see page 16), hold a large handful of moss against the wire circle and secure the moss in place by wrapping the spool wire or monofilament around it several times in 1½- to 2-inch intervals (see Figure 6). Continue adding handfuls of moss until the entire wire circle is covered and you are satisfied with the shape and thickness of the base.

Moss also can be used to fill the multiple-wire ring bases available in craft stores. These ring bases have a small trench that encircles the base and can be filled with natural materials, such as sweet Annie, artemisia, and moss. Pack the base with the moss (see Figure 7 on page 20); you can use fresh moss and let it dry in place. Secure the moss by wrapping a length of monofilament or medium-gauge floral wire at 2-inch intervals around the wire base.

Another way to use moss on a base is as part of a three-dimensional construction. This approach gives you a surface area on another plane on which materials can be placed. Simply cut a square of dry floral foam to the desired size and attach it to a vine base with floral wire and/or hot glue (see Figure 8 on page 20). Cover the floral

*Figure 5*

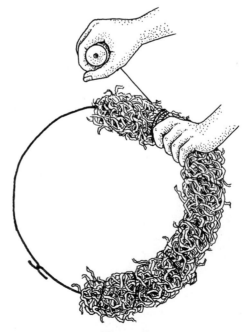

*Figure 6*

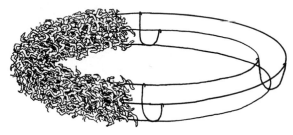

*Figure 7*

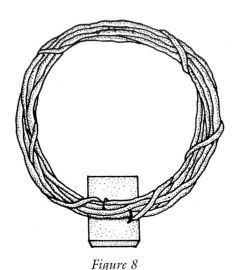

*Figure 8*

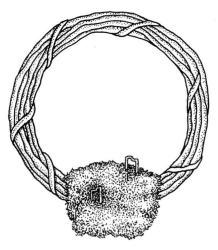

*Figure 9*

foam with a piece of sheet moss, using floral picks or pins to secure it (see Figure 9). Then use floral picks or hot glue to attach materials as you would with a polystyrene base (see "Wreaths" on page 236).

## Wet Floral Foam Bases

The dense green foam from which these bases are made retains water so that any fresh-cut materials inserted into the base will be kept moist. (To prevent moisture from staining the surface on which the finished wreath is placed, most wet foam bases are backed with an impermeable plastic material. For extra protection, place a sheet of glass or acrylic plastic under the wreath.) These wreaths can be purchased through a florist, or you can make your own by purchasing floral foam in squares (available at craft-supply stores) and using a serrated knife to cut pieces to fit the trench in a multiple-wire base. Using thin floral tape, secure the foam to the base.

## Polystyrene Bases

Man-made polystyrene bases are relatively inexpensive, lightweight, and sturdier than you might imagine. Unless they've been adorned, they're fairly unattractive, so it's important to completely cover these bases with your background material.

To make your own polystyrene base, purchase a few blocks of this material from a craft-supply store, arm yourself with a serrated knife, and cut the desired shape. Then completely cover the base with moss as described in "Moss-Covered Bases" on page 19.

## Wire Bases

With nothing more than a pair of wire cutters and some heavy-gauge floral wire or an old coat hanger, you'll be able to make bases for swags, garlands, and wreaths. Just cut the wire 4 inches longer than you want the finished base to be. Overlap the ends by 2 inches and fasten your circle by wrapping the remaining length of wire around the overlapped ends.

# WREATH BASE OPTIONS

### Vine

*Advantages*

Complements many different wreath designs; so attractive that large portions can be left uncovered; can be purchased or easily made in a wide range of sizes, shapes, and materials; can be painted any color; sturdy enough to support heavy items; gives the wreath a natural look.

*Drawbacks*

A large vine base is heavy compared to other bases.

*Attachment Methods*

Use hot glue and/or floral wire; wire on large items, such as fruits and novelties; working with the vine's weave, you can insert a pick at an angle into the spaces between the vines after a dab of hot glue has been placed on the end of the pick.

### Straw

*Advantages*

Offers a permeable frame on which to attach any type of material; commercial ones tend to be densely packed and reinforced with wire, making them perfect for heavy items; good for full, lush wreath designs; appearance can be altered by covering the base with moss, fabric, or ribbon, which also creates a surface more receptive to hot glue.

*Drawbacks*

Base's bulk does not suit dainty, delicate wreath styles; need to cover all of the base with materials.

*Attachment Methods*

Use floral picks and/or floral pins; larger items, such as fruits or novelties, can be attached with wire or hot glue.

*(continued on next page)*

# WREATH BASE OPTIONS—CONTINUED

### Moss

*Advantages*

Easy to hot-glue items to surface, to pick in flowers, and to insert single stems of flowers or greenery; so attractive that large portions can be left uncovered; easy to make; gives the wreath a natural look.

*Drawbacks*

Not very strong unless the moss is covering a straw base; rustic look can be unsuitable for certain designs and decor.

*Attachment Methods*

Use floral picks and/or hot glue; insert single stems of flowers and greenery directly into the base.

### Polystyrene

*Advantages*

Inexpensive and available in more varieties of thickness, size, and shape than any other type of base; color and surface texture can be altered by wrapping with ribbon or covering with moss or leaves; available with a mirror in the center; larger wire-reinforced bases are available to accommodate heavy materials.

*Drawbacks*

Beauty of the finished wreath is diminished if any small gaps reveal the polystyrene base; some hot glues are hot enough to melt the polystyrene; not very sturdy unless reinforced with wire.

*Attachment Methods*

Cover with ribbon or moss secured with floral pins, then attach small items with cool-melt glue.

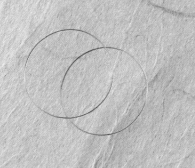

### Single-Wire Ring

*Advantages*

Works well with delicate designs using lightweight materials; can be covered with bunches of materials, such as artemisia or greens, or covered with moss to give the base a broader surface on which to attach flowers.

*Drawbacks*

Can't accommodate heavy items; all of the base must be covered with materials; hard to work with because materials tend to slip on the surface.

*Attachment Methods*

Cover the wire with bunches of plant material wrapped with monofilament and then attach them using hot glue or fine-gauge wire.

## Multiple-Wire Ring

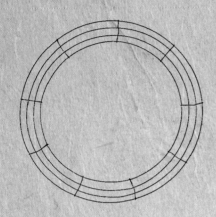

### Advantages

Inner trench can be packed with natural materials or wet floral foam to provide an area in which other materials can nest.

### Drawbacks

Can't support heavy items; essentially a specialty base with limited design applications.

*Attachment Methods*

Cover with plant materials secured with monofilament and then attach them using hot glue or fine-gauge floral wire; fill the trench with moss, pine needles, or herbs, and then use hot glue to attach the natural materials; if the wreath will hang on a wall, secure the materials inside the trench with monofilament or thin-gauge floral wire, and then glue on the materials; or fill the trench with wet floral foam held in place with floral tape, and then pick in materials or insert the stems into the foam.

## Double-Wire Ring

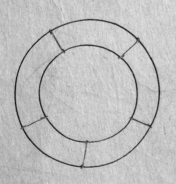

### Advantages

When covered with decorative paper or ribbon, creates a flat, wide surface, perfect for attaching large, delicate materials that would break if wound around the curves of a foam, vine, or straw base.

### Drawbacks

Can't support heavy items; essentially a specialty base with limited design applications.

*Attachment Methods*

Wrap colored paper or ribbon around both rings and attach it with hot glue; cover with plant materials secured with monofilament and then attach them using hot glue or fine-gauge floral wire.

# BASKETS

Just about everyone seems to know some-one who collects baskets. What is the fasci-nation with these beautiful and practical objects? Baskets are perhaps one of the oldest nature crafts—they have been made by people of different civilizations for hun-dreds of years. We can easily imagine the many practical uses our hunter-gatherer ancestors had for baskets. Later, baskets served as traps for game and fish and as carrying and storage containers for farmers. They were made from any wood, vine, leaf, or fiber that could be formed into work-able shapes.

Although we no longer rely on baskets for carrying and storage, basketry has remained a popular functional and decora-tive craft. In fact, the trend in collecting early baskets has turned old relics into expensive antiques. Perhaps some day your woven work of art will become the cher-ished treasure of a future basket collector.

## Basketry Materials

Baskets are still made from common natu-ral materials. But because of the increased number of basket makers and the scarcity of native woods, we now import more and more supplies, particularly rattan core, which is usually referred to as reed. To a large extent, flat reed has replaced oak, ash, and hickory splints, and round reed has replaced oak, willow, and other vinelike materials used for ribbed or twined baskets. Reed is readily available in a wide range of sizes and quantities from craft-, hobby-, weaving-, and basket-supply stores, and from mail-order suppliers. Although some basket makers still harvest their own oak and other hardwoods, you can buy oak splints and other wood for baskets through some basket-supply stores and mail-order suppliers (see "Supply Sources" on page 254). You can also make baskets from grasses, bark, pine needles, twigs, and vines that you collect yourself.

## Basket Shapes and Techniques

The basket shapes we use today have been passed along to us from our long-ago rela-tives; the well-known egg, potato, and melon baskets were originally designed by basket makers in Ireland, Wales, Scotland, and England. Several of the basket projects you'll find in this section are based on these tried-and-true designs. For example, the "Iris & Willow Potato Basket" on page 35 is a charming rendition of this popular shape. The original potato basket was used during the harvest to gather potatoes and was designed to be dragged through the rows while hold-ing a great deal of weight. It uses a ribbed construction made by first shaping a sturdy frame that establishes the intended form before you start weaving. Most are begun with one or two hoops for a rim and handle; ribs are inserted into the hoop lashings to form arcs that outline the shape of the basket. Weavers are then threaded over and under the ribs and back and forth between the rims. Other types of basket construction include plaited (see "Catch-All Basket" on page 32) and coiled (see "Pine-Needle Basket" on page 184 in the chapter on pine needles).

## Soaking Basketry Materials

It is best to work with moist and flexible material, achieved by soaking it in warm water. Depending on its thickness, you may need to soak the material for 3 to 30 minutes. Don't let it soak for more than that without checking its condition, or you will wind up with reed or oak that is likely to fray or split when you weave it. If, after 5 minutes, a thin reed weaver feels flexible, it is ready to be removed from the water. Keep your damp materials in a towel or plastic bag while you weave.

## Dyeing Basketry Materials

Combining colored weaving material with natural material can give a basket a very beautiful look. You can dye basketry materials with basketry, fabric, or commercial dyes, following the directions on the package.

Start with one-quarter of the amount you've purchased, dissolved in two quarts of almost boiling water. The temperature of the water is very important to successful dyeing; be sure it reaches near boiling. Use a small piece of basketry material to test the shade, leaving it in for about 30 seconds. If the dye bath isn't strong enough, add more dye (up to the entire amount you've bought). If it's too dark, add more water. When the sample piece is the desired color, coil the presoaked basketry material into a loose ring and submerge it in the dye bath for 30 to 45 seconds. Remove it from the dye, allow it to dry (which will help the color set), then rinse it in very hot water until the water runs clear. Another way to help set the color is to soak the dyed reed for 30 to 60 minutes in warm water to which you've added one cup of white vinegar.

To achieve a more natural appearance, use a stain made from walnut hulls. Use the entire nut with the hull. Place the hulls in a nylon pouch or a pair of old stockings and cover them with water. In a few days, you will have a lovely brown stain. For quick results, boil the hulls in water and immediately dip your materials in the stain. For other dye techniques that give oak a natural look, see "White Oak Cat-Head Basket" on page 39.

## Basketry Tools

There are a few tools and supplies that are required for nearly every basket you will make. They include:

- Awl
- Basketry clippers or pruning shears (with a soft, plastic handle and narrow tips)
- Clothespins
- Large bucket or pail
- Scissors
- Sharp pencil
- Sharp pocketknife or craft knife
- Spray bottle filled with water
- Tape measure
- Yardstick

## Weaving Variations

All baskets, no matter what their shape or what type of material they are made from, are woven—meaning that one set of materials is interlaced with another. The warp is the stationary element. When you're working with flat reed, the warp is the stake, and the weft is the weaver. With round reed, the warp is the spoke, and the weft is still the weaver. For definitions and illustrations of specific basketry terms, see the "Basket-Making Glossary" on page 28. The "Basket Weave Variations" chart on page 26 defines and illustrates the basic forms, listed in the order of the most commonly used variations.

## Getting Started

Now it's your turn to make a basket. The projects in this section range from simple to challenging and offer a good representation of different weaving techniques and basket construction. As with many crafts, trial and error is your best ally in learning. With a few basic tools and patient, nimble fingers, you will soon be making great-looking baskets.

# BASKET WEAVE VARIATIONS

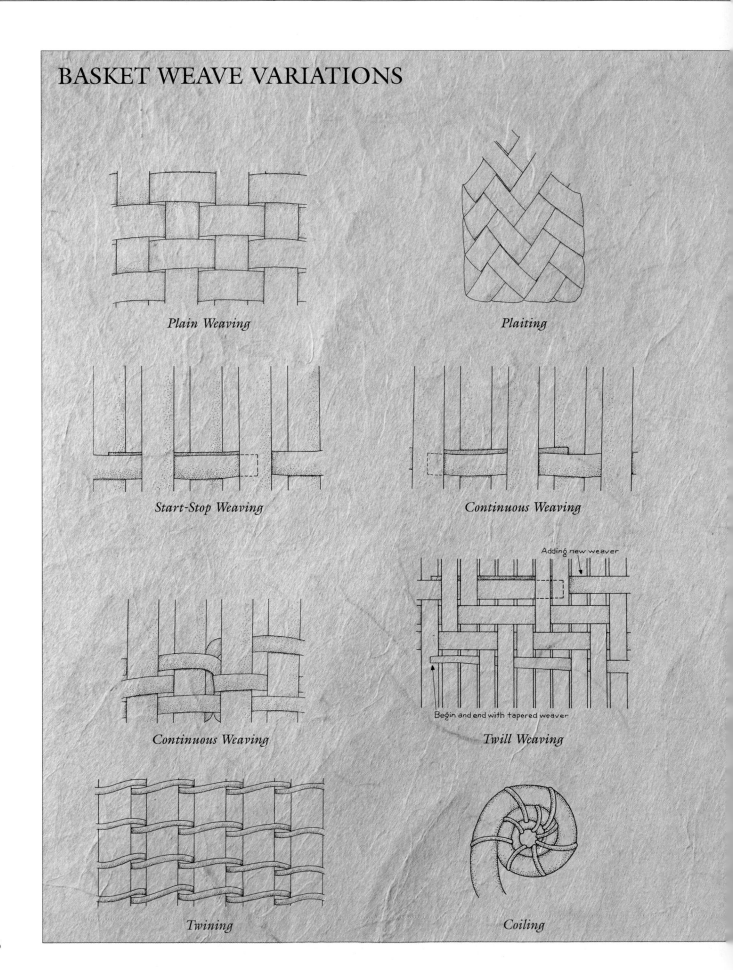

*Plain Weaving*

*Plaiting*

*Start-Stop Weaving*

*Continuous Weaving*

*Continuous Weaving*

Adding new weaver

Begin and end with tapered weaver

*Twill Weaving*

*Twining*

*Coiling*

**Plain Weaving** • The simplest and most common form of weaving, done with rigid stakes or spokes and weavers that wrap around the stakes in an over-one-under-one pattern. When using round reed, this is called randing.

**Plaiting** • The term used in basketry for the interlacing of two flat materials of equal width. Diagonal plaiting is plain weaving with two similar materials interwoven at right angles.

**Start-Stop Weaving** • Refers to weaving around a base one row at a time, starting and stopping each row. With your flat reed, begin the weaver on the outside of the basket on the outside of a stake. Weave around the basket and end by weaving over and beyond the starting point, cutting the weaver behind the fourth stake.

**Continuous Weaving** • Weaving done continuously from beginning to end, weaving over the starting point indefinitely, with weavers added periodically. There are several methods of adding new weavers. Working with flat reed, a new weaver is slipped in under the fourth stake from the end of the old weaver (see Figure 4). With round reed, the new weaver is added by tucking it down between two stakes after an over or under stroke.

**Twill Weaving** • A method of weaving in which a weaver passes over two or more stakes or spokes and under one or more stakes or spokes.

**Twining** • Usually done with round reed, worked over or around either flat or round reed, with a half-twist at each crossing. It is often used as a locking row around flat bases to hold the stakes in place.

**Arrow Weaving** • A decorative form of twining, often used to create a simple woven border (see Figures 8, 9, and 10 of the "Catch-All Basket" on page 32).

**Coiling** • The technique of wrapping a foundation of fibers with thread or other materials into a ropelike strand that is then stitched in concentric circles.

# BASKET-MAKING GLOSSARY

**Base**      The bottom of the basket.

**Butt**      To bring the ends of any two pieces together, flush against each other.

**Ear**       The lashing used to secure the intersection of the basket's rim and handle; also the lashing into which the basket's ribs are inserted.

**Filling-in**   The back-and-forth weaving done to fill in a wedge-shaped area that may remain unwoven on a ribbed basket; also called gussetting.

**Lasher**    The piece of reed that wraps around the rim of the basket, securing the rim to the top of the sides.

**Packing**   Pushing each row snugly down beside the previously woven row.

**Reed**      The inner core of the rattan palm that has been cut into flat, round, oval, half-round, or half-oval shapes.

**Ribs**      The round or oval pieces that extend from one side of the basket to the other and form the skeleton of a ribbed basket.

**Rims**      The pieces, inside and out, that fit over the top row of weaving to form an edge and give stability to the sides.

**Spokes**    The materials, usually round reed, which form the base and the rigid framework of a basket—the equivalent of stakes.

**Stakes**    The elements that are woven to form the base and then are upsett or gently turned up to become the upright materials around which the basket is woven.

**True**      To measure the woven base, making sure all the sides are the correct length and adjusting them if necessary.

**Upsett**    To bend the basket's stakes up after the base is completed to create vertical elements for weaving the sides.

**Warp**      The stationary, usually more rigid, element in weaving; a stake or spoke.

**Weaver**    The flexible fiber used to weave over and under the stakes, spokes, or ribs.

**Weft**      The more flexible weaving element that is interlaced around the warp; the weaver.

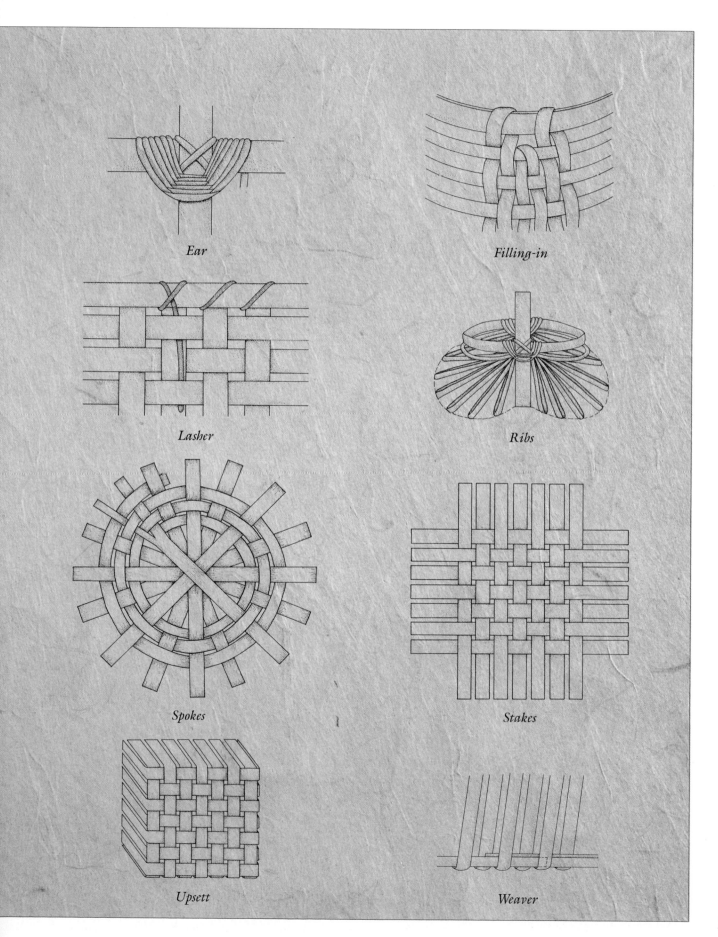

Ear

Filling-in

Lasher

Ribs

Spokes

Stakes

Upsett

Weaver

*These handy baskets are attractive and simple to make. By adding more spokes, you can weave one large enough to store onions. The twining weave is very versatile and almost any shape can be achieved once the basic technique is mastered.*

# Garlic Basket

## What You Need

100 yards of #4 round reed

Large bucket

Basketry, fabric, or commercial dye in your choice of color

Basketry clippers or pruning shears

## What You Do

*1* Dye your reed in the bucket following the directions in "Dyeing Basketry Materials" on page 25. Then soak all of the dyed reed in warm water for 20 minutes or until it is pliable.

*2* Cut six pieces of round reed, each 36 inches long, to use for spokes. Place three reeds over and perpendicular to the other three at their centers. Begin the base by twining a long piece of reed (at least 50 inches) over and under the six spokes, alternately, making three revolutions (see Figure 1).

**3** As you begin the fourth revolution, continue to twine, but this time open out each spoke like a wheel and upsett the twining by creating a half twist between one spoke and then a pair of spokes, going over and under them (see Figure 2).

**4** You will be shaping the sides of the basket by gently turning the spokes up as you twine. Twine up the basket three times around. Keep the weaving flat by creating a ¼-inch space between each round of twining, exposing the spokes. Keep the spacing even between each row. End each weaver by tucking the ends into the weaving beside a spoke. Each weaver will alternately appear on the inside and then on the outside of the basket as the work moves in a spiral form from the base to the rim.

**5** Now you are ready to begin your simple closed border. Soak the spokes for five minutes or until they are pliable. Weave the shaded spoke, marked 1, under spoke 2, then over spokes 3 and 4, to the inside of the basket (see Figure 3). The rule is "under a spoke, over two spokes, and in." Go around the basket until all of the spokes are woven to the inside, then clip them closely against a spoke. A hanger can be tied on now by coiling a short piece of reed and weaving the ends through the basket border until they are secure.

*Note:* An easy adaptation is the onion storage basket. Add six more spokes and enlarge the base until it is about 6 inches in diameter. Twine up the side for 8 inches and finish the basket with a closed border.

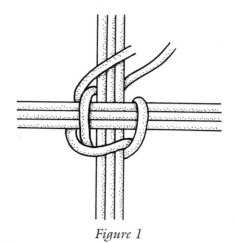

*Figure 1*

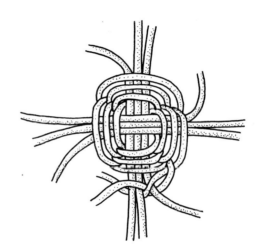

*Figure 2*

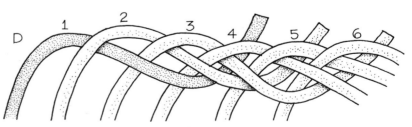

*Figure 3*

*The designer intended this basket to catch mail or messages, but it's perfect as a napkin holder.*

# Catch-All Basket

## WHAT YOU NEED

13.3 yards of #2 round reed

1 D-handle, 8 × 12 inches
 (available at basket-supply stores)

21.6 yards of flat reed, ⅜ inch wide

1 yard of ash, 1 inch wide

9 yards of flat or flat-oval reed,
 ¹¹⁄₆₄ inch wide

2 yards of flat-oval reed, ½ inch wide

1 yard of #2 or #3 sea grass

Tape measure

Basketry clippers or pruning shears

2 large buckets

Basketry, fabric, or commercial dyes
 in burgundy and dark green

Sandpaper

Pencil

4 to 6 clothespins

Sharp pocketknife or craft knife

## WHAT YOU DO

1 Soak 8 yards of #2 round reed in warm water for five to ten minutes. Dye 4 yards with the burgundy dye, following the directions in "Dyeing Basketry Materials" on page 25. Repeat this process with the other 4 yards of reed and the dark green dye.

2 Sand the D-handle. Measure the bottom of it (from side to side) and make a pencil mark in the center. From the ⅜-inch-wide flat reed, cut four pieces 28 inches long and nine pieces 26 inches long. Mark the center of each piece on the rough side. Soak all the pieces in warm

water for five to ten minutes until they are pliable. Lay the four 28-inch pieces as shown in Figure 1, aligning all the center marks. Leave about half an inch between the pieces. Beginning with the center piece, weave the shorter pieces of flat reed through in plain weave. The center marks of both center pieces should align. The woven base should resemble Figure 2 and measure approximately $4\frac{1}{2} \times 7\frac{1}{2}$ inches.

3 Soak a long piece of undyed #2 round reed in warm water for five to ten minutes until it is pliable and twine around the base for two rows. Treat the handle as a stake and twine around it also, even though it is upright. At this point, there is a top weaver and a bottom weaver. The top weaver goes under the next stake and continues to do so. Figure 3 shows the beginning of twining. When you reach the starting point, continue twining around the base again. End the twining after the second row by tucking the ends under the two twined rows, one at a time, on two successive stakes, as shown in Figure 4.

4 Upsett all the stakes by bending them over onto themselves toward the inside of the basket, as shown in Figure 5. They will not stand upright, but more importantly, a crease has been made at the base of each stake.

5 Soak one piece of $\frac{3}{8}$-inch-wide flat reed in warm water for five to ten minutes until it is pliable. Begin by placing the end of the reed on the outside of the center of either the front or the back of the basket, and weave over one stake and under the next, making every other stake upright as you weave around it. To check yourself, make sure the weaver goes under the handle on the first row. Leave the "unders" lying down, as you will weave around them and make them stand on the next row. Pinch the weaver at the corners on the first row. On subsequent rows, let the weavers "round" the corners with no pinch. End the first and all rows as shown in Figure 6 on page 34, by weaving over the beginning of the piece to the fourth stake. Cut the weaver and start the next

row on another side of the basket. Weave over the stakes that were "unders" on the last row. Repeat these two rows until there is a total of five rows around the basket.

6 Soak a long piece of each color of the dyed #2 round reed in warm water for five to ten minutes until they are pliable. Place the end of one color behind any stake and the end of the other colored reed behind the next stake. Twine around the basket as shown in Figure 7 on page 34, ending on the stake before the starting stake. Make a "step-up" by moving the farthest right weaver over one stake to the right, behind the next, and out to the front. Move the other weaver over one stake to the right, behind the next one, and out to the front, as shown in Figure 8 on page 34. This is the first part of a decorative twining called arrow weave.

7 Now, do one row of reverse twining, but this time move the left weaver under the right weaver and behind the next stake. Repeat with each "left" weaver. End the row of reverse twining as shown in Figure 9 on page 34, taking the ends of both weavers behind the beginning spokes and going under the weaving already in place. Figure 10 on page 34 shows the two rows completed, creating one band of arrow weave. Next, weave in one row of the soaked 1-inch-wide ash in regular plain weave. Repeat the entire procedure with two more pieces of dyed #2 round reed to make two more rows of arrow weave. Then weave four rows of plain weave with the $\frac{3}{8}$-inch-wide flat reed.

8 To make the back of the basket higher than the front, you must weave several rows of $\frac{11}{64}$-inch-wide flat or flat oval reed to gradually build the height in back. With a sharp knife, taper the end of one long piece of soaked $\frac{11}{64}$-inch-wide reed for about 5 inches, making it little more than threadlike at the beginning and gradually becoming wider until it reaches its normal width.

9 Hold the basket in your hands and look at the front. Turn the basket

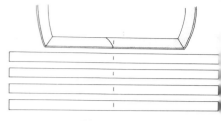

*Figure 1*

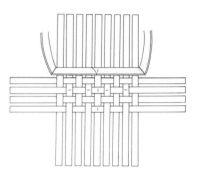

*Figure 2*

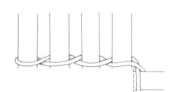

*Figure 3*

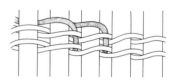

*Figure 4*

*Figure 5*

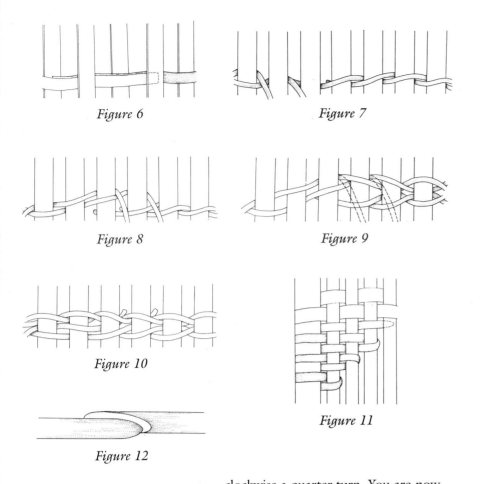

*Figure 6*

*Figure 7*

*Figure 8*

*Figure 9*

*Figure 10*

*Figure 11*

*Figure 12*

*Figure 13*

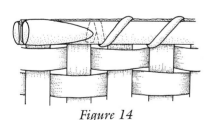

*Figure 14*

clockwise a quarter turn. You are now looking at the right end of the basket. Designate the 1st stake on the left side as stake 1 and mentally number the others all the way around to the last stake on the other end. The 5th stake is the handle on the one side, as is the 15th on the other side. The last stake is the 19th. Start the tapered weaver behind stake 1 and weave over and under all the way around the basket to stake 19 on the other side. Turn the weaver around stake 19 and return, still weaving over and under, until you reach stake 2 on the first side. This time, turn the weaver around stake 2 and weave back to stake 18 on the other side. Turn again and return to stake 3. On each successive row you skip the next numbered stake, which means you weave around one fewer stake. You continue to skip one stake until there are only nine stakes left to weave around on the back of the basket. Make a turn around each end-stake, taper the end of the

weaver until it is threadlike, and end it behind the 1st stake, as shown in Figure 11. Then, with a long piece of soaked #2 round reed, twine three rows around the top of the basket. End the pieces by tucking the ends into the twining.

**10** For the rim, measure a piece of ½-inch-wide flat oval reed that is long enough to circle the top of the basket twice, plus about 6 inches for overlap, and cut the piece in half. Soak the two pieces in warm water for five or ten minutes until they are pliable. Place one piece around the inside of the basket, covering the three rows of twining. Hold it in place with clothespins and allow the ends to overlap 2 to 3 inches. Mark the reed, top and bottom, where the overlap occurs. With the second piece, repeat the procedure on the outside of the basket, again covering the three rows of twining, securing the reed with clothespins, and marking the place where the overlap occurs.

**11** Remove the two pieces of reed and bevel the ends with a sharp knife so that the overlapped area is no thicker than a single piece of ½-inch-wide flat oval, as shown in Figure 12. Reposition the two rim pieces on the basket. Place the splices (overlapped areas) near but not opposite each other, as shown in Figure 13. Hold them in place with clothespins.

**12** Place the piece of sea grass between the two rim pieces. With a long, soaked piece of ¹¹⁄₆₄-inch-wide reed, begin lashing the rim pieces together, as shown in Figure 14. Push the end of the reed up under the inside rim, over the wall of the basket, and down to the outside. The end can be cut later, flush with the bottom of the rim. Take the lasher into every space between the stakes. When the starting point is reached, either reverse the direction of the lashing and X-lash, or end after a single row the same way it began by hooking the end of the lasher over the basket wall, or hide the end behind a weaver inside the basket.

# Iris & Willow Potato Basket

## WHAT YOU NEED

2 strips of dried bark, 1/3 × 25 inches

4 willow twigs, 1/3 × 36 inches

18 willow twigs, 1/4 to 1/3 × 25 inches

15 to 20 weeping-willow twigs,
   1/8 × 30 inches

125 dried iris leaves

Large bucket

Old towel

Tape measure

Basketry clippers or pruning shears

Sharp pocketknife or craft knife

## WHAT YOU DO

*1* Reconstitute your dried bark and iris leaves by soaking them in warm water for 15 to 20 minutes or until they are flexible. Wrap them in a damp towel to absorb the extra moisture.

*2* Using the four 36-inch-long willow twigs, fashion a hoop 9 inches in diameter (see "Making a Vine Wreath Base" on page 18 for instructions on making a grapevine wreath base). This hoop is your basket rim.

*3* Cut three of the 25-inch-long willow twigs so that each is 22 inches long. Hold the hoop and place one of these

*Potato baskets were once used to drag the harvest in from the fields. This smaller version uses variegated colors and textures for a new take on a traditional form.*

35

*Random weaving,*
*shown to eye-catching*
*effect in this platter,*
*is more sculptural*
*than technical. It is*
*best undertaken after*
*you have made more*
*traditional baskets*
*and are comfortable*
*with basketry-*
*weaving techniques.*

# Random-Weave Platter

## WHAT YOU NEED

33 yards of #7 round reed

50 to 75 yards of flat reed, ¾ inch wide

Basketry, fabric, or commercial dyes in
    your choice of 2 or 3 colors

Large bucket

Basketry clippers or pruning shears

## WHAT YOU DO

*1* Dye all of the round and flat reed following the directions in "Dyeing
Basketry Materials" on page 25. Dye the
flat reed all one color and the round reed
two or three complementary colors.

*2* Soak all of the dyed round reed in
warm water for 20 minutes or until it
is pliable. Use it to form a basket rim 13
inches in diameter by coiling the reed
around itself three times. Cut the end and
tuck it into the coil.

*3* Clip the rest of the round reed as
needed to lengths that are comfortable
for you to work with, such as 4 feet or
longer. Start the body of the basket by
crossing one length of round reed through
any single strand of the coiled rim and
across to the opposite side of the rim.

Crisscross a few times through the rim and
down across the bottom and then back
through the rim. The reed, with its round
shape, will curve naturally into a shallow
bowl or platter shape; you won't have to
bend it. Weave a few more lengths of round
reed into the body without connecting it to
the rim, weaving over, under, and around the
original diagonals in a random fashion, creating a fairly flat platter shape.

*4* Soak the flat reed for 20 minutes or until it
is pliable. You can clip the reed as needed
to lengths ranging from 7 to 12 inches, or you
can work with 4-foot lengths and clip the ends
as you weave. Weave lengths of flat reed into
the basket body, going over and under the
round reeds. Keep covering up the holes in the
random weaving, but do not go back over the
same areas. Use as much flat reed as you like
until your platter has a form.

*5* With the round reed, fill in any spaces
that seem to need it. To give the basket
a flat base, push it down on a table top while
the reed is still damp.

*6* Fasten the basket body to the coiled rim
by untwining some of the round reed
from the woven body and wrapping it around
the rim and back to the body again. Clip any
unsightly reed ends; clip them close to the body
and on the underside, if possible.

# White Oak Cat-Head Basket

## WHAT YOU NEED

50 yards of split or shaved white oak weavers, $\frac{1}{8}$ inch wide and $\frac{3}{100}$ inch thick

1 rim of split or shaved white oak, 27 inches long, shaved round, and $\frac{3}{16}$ inch wide

18 stakes of split or shaved white oak, 25 inches long, $\frac{3}{8}$ inch wide, and $\frac{1}{25}$ inch thick

2 rims of half-round oak, 26 inches long and $\frac{3}{8}$ inch wide

2 blocks of wood (any kind), $5\frac{1}{2}$ inches square and $\frac{1}{4}$ to $\frac{1}{2}$ inch wide

1 tablespoon of iron (ferrous) sulfate (available in drugstores)

Enamel or stainless steel pot

Large bucket

5- to 6-inch-diameter round container with straight sides

Spool of string

Scissors

4 to 6 clothespins

Awl or small screwdriver

Sharp pocketknife or craft knife

Tape measure

Spray bottle filled with water

6-inch-diameter bowl

Electric drill with $\frac{1}{16}$-inch drill bit

Curved upholstery needle

Spool of navy waxed-linen thread

Fingernail clipper

Basketry clippers or pruning shears

*This basket seems to have originated with the Shakers and derives its name from its resemblance—when turned upside down—to a cat's head.*

## WHAT YOU DO

*1* Dye blue all 50 yards of the $\frac{1}{8}$-inch-wide weavers and the 27-inch-long rim as follows: In the enamel or stainless steel pot, heat to almost boiling a mixture of one teaspoon iron sulfate dissolved in a gallon of water. (The amount of iron sulfate you need is approximate because the chemical content of water varies across the country.)

*2* Immerse the weavers and rim in the dye bath. The tannic acid in oak acts as a mordant to fix the dye. If you are cutting your own oak, be sure to cut it to the desired width before you dye it; if it's cut after you dye it, there will be a white edge

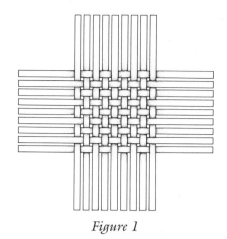

*Figure 1*

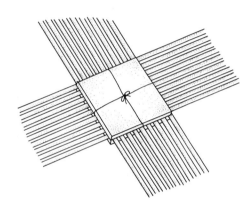

*Figure 2*

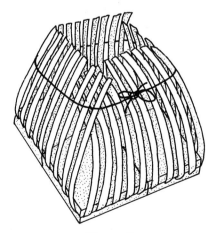

*Figure 3*

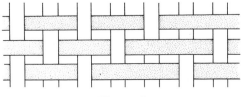

*Figure 4*

on the oak. Check the color after about 15 minutes. The dye bath usually takes one to two hours. Remember that the oak will look darker when it is wet; heartwood will dye darker than sapwood. When you are happy with the color, rinse the oak until the water runs clear and let the oak dry before using it.

3 Soak the 18 undyed stakes in clear warm water for 30 minutes or until they are moist and pliable.

4 Soak the two natural-colored rims of half-round oak in clear, warm water for 30 to 60 minutes. When they are pliable, roll them, one with the flat side in and one with the flat side out. Put them in the round container and let the rims dry in this position; this makes it easier to work with them. Repeat this process with the blue rim.

5 To form the base, place nine soaked stakes on a table, about ⅜ inch apart, with their ends aligned. Weave the other nine stakes over and under them, making sure the weaving is alternated in each row (see Figure 1). Measure and true the base to a 5½-inch square. Place the basket base on top of one of the 5½-inch blocks of wood. Make sure the woven bottom fits the block exactly. Place the other block on top and tightly tie the blocks around the woven base with string (see Figure 2).

6 Pull the stakes up very gently, bending each one upward; do not fold or crease them. Tie the stakes together with string so they dry in a pleasing shape (see Figure 3). Make the effort now to position the stakes so that all the sides look evenly sloped; if one side is uneven at this stage, it will be very hard to make the basket symmetrical as you proceed. If necessary, use clothespins to hold the string and stakes in place.

7 When the stakes are dry, remove the clothespins and string, but leave the wooden squares in place. Start weaving at a corner; tuck the end of a weaver under a corner stake and weave over-under-over. When you reach the starting stake again, skip over two stakes and continue weaving. Each time around, you must go under the first stake that you skipped in the previous row, and again skip over two stakes; this creates an upwardly spiraling pattern around

the four corners at the bottom of the basket (see Figure 4). Make sure the oval side of the weaver is on the outside of the basket. Complete three rows in this way. When one weaver is used up, cut it off on top of a stake. Unravel the weaver back several stakes. With a sharp knife, peel off some wood from the underside of both this weaver and the new weaver. Overlap the four stakes. The new weaver should blend right in. As these three rows are woven, pull the corner stakes toward each other.

**8** After these three rows of weaving, remove the wooden squares. Weave now in a basic over-under-over pattern. As you weave, be sure to pull the corners toward each other to begin the shaping of the cat-head bottom. There are two ways you can shape the basket: One technique is to pull the corner stakes together while weaving flat; this bows the sides up. The second technique is to mist the bottom with water to soften the oak. Put your knee in the center of the bottom from the outside and mash the bottom around your knee frequently as you weave.

**9** The curved sides of this basket should come out and up very gradually (see Figure 5). When the side of the basket is 1 inch high, you should have woven about 11 rows; several of the first rows do not rise vertically. The circumference at the top should now be 29 inches, with a base circumference of 22 inches. At 2 inches high,

the circumference should be 31½ inches. From 2 inches to 4 inches high, the circumference should stay about the same to give a straight look to the sides.

**10** Rewet your stakes with water from the spray bottle and gently pull them in toward the center of the basket. Tie them together at the top to form a tepee shape. Allow the stakes to dry. Pack the weavers by inserting the awl or screwdriver in between two stakes and pushing the weaver down against the one below it. Continue weaving until you get the sides back up to 4 inches. As you weave, push the stakes toward the center of the basket to decrease the circumference; continue to pack the weavers down tightly.

**11** Rewet the stakes with water from the spray bottle and wedge the small bowl inside the basket to straighten the stakes (see Figure 6). When the stakes are dry, remove the bowl and repack the weavers. Weave until the basket is 6¼ inches high with a circumference of about 22½ inches. You are now ready to finish off the weaving. To make the top level, weave until you reach the stake where you first started weaving. For a distance of five to six stakes, gradually reduce the width of the weavers you are using until you are weaving with one that is the width of a thread. Weave the end of that one behind a stake.

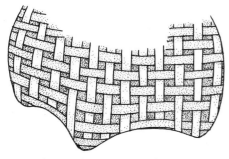

*Figure 5*

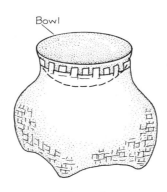

*Figure 6*

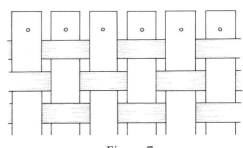

*Figure 7*

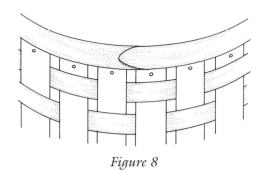

*Figure 8*

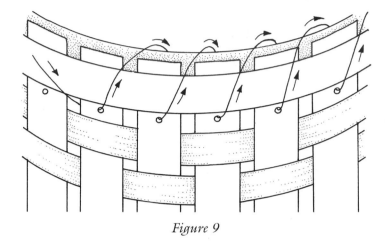

*Figure 9*

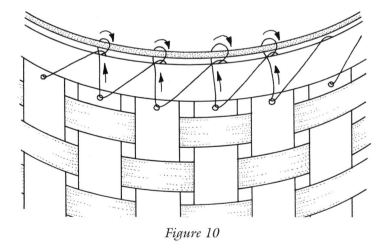

*Figure 10*

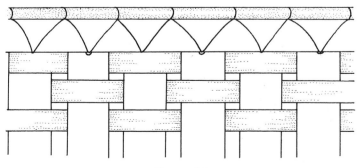

*Figure 11*

*12* With the drill, make holes in each stake just above the last row of weavers. Cut the stakes at right angles about ⅜ inch above this last row of weaving (see Figure 7 on page 41). The stakes must not be higher than the rim. With a clothespin, hold the natural-colored rims in place, with the flat sides of the rims against the stakes. Overlap the ends of the rims 2 to 2½ inches. With a knife, trim down the overlaps on the sides that touch so that the total thickness of the overlap is the same as the original thickness of the rim (see Figure 8).

*13* Thread the curved needle with a long piece of the waxed-linen thread and sew the rims onto the basket. Leave a 2-inch-long tail of thread to tie to the end of the thread when you are finished sewing. Starting at the back of the stake, come through the hole, around the rim, behind the stake, and through the hole of the next stake (see Figure 9). When the rim is sewn on, go back through the first hole in preparation to sew on the round, blue rim.

*14* Use clothespins to hold the rim in place (it should be trimmed in the same manner as the natural-colored rim so that the overlap is tapered). The lashing is now reversed; at the top of the natural-colored rim, go under the linen thread that is there. Go behind the blue rim, over the top to the front, under the linen thread again, behind the natural-colored rim, and into the next hole to the left (see Figures 10 and 11).

*15* To tie off the threads, knot the 2-inch-long tail of thread hanging inside the basket and use the curved needle to weave it over a stake or two. Cut it close and mash it against another strand of thread; the wax will hold the threads in place. Use the fingernail clipper to clip away any "hairs" that may be on the basket.

***For more information on gathering these materials and for specific basket projects,*** see "Bark" on page 10, "Pine Needles" on page 182, "Twigs" on page 221, and "Vines" on page 231.

# BERRIES

The ever-popular red holly berry conjures up warm remembrances of the winter holidays; but don't think of berries as appropriate only for Christmas nature crafts. Berries can be delightful decorative accents at any time of the year.

Berries provide the nature crafter with attractive components for many types of projects, including wreaths, centerpieces, and topiaries. They come in a variety of sizes and colors: plump, red cranberries; tiny, pink pepperberries; variegated orange bittersweet berries; delicate, light green eucalyptus berries; and subtle teal spruce berries. All of these berries can provide just the right touch to many floral projects, and they combine well with projects using fruits and vegetables.

Many popular berries, such as pepperberries and canella berries, are available at craft-supply stores. Canella berries are often dyed in a range of colors to match your palette. But a simple stroll through your backyard may reward you with an array of berries free for the picking. Berries grow singly, on separate stalks, in umbrella formations, and in other kinds of clusters. They grow on herbs, woody plants with needles, woody plants with broad leaves, vines and creeping shrubs, small trees, and many other locations.

You can use the berries fresh, or you can pick them and let them air-dry (see "Air Drying" on page 73). Berries are also available in silk and plastic versions, and their colors and textures can fool even the loyal naturalist. Many designers mix in a few artificial berries with the real thing, as the "Holiday Wreath" on page 44 magnificently demonstrates.

Berries can be hot-glued onto your project individually or in groups, but the easiest way to attach berries to a floral project, such as a wreath or a swag, is to hot-glue or wire them to a floral pick in small clusters.

## Popular Berries for Craft Projects

- Bayberries
- Blackberries
- Blueberries
- Cannella berries
- Cranberries
- Holly berries
- Juniper berries
- Mistletoe
- Pepperberries
- Spruce berries

## Don't Touch!

When you come across a plant and each of its leaves has three leaflets and the berries are smooth, the plant is poison ivy; if the berries are hairy, the plant is poison oak. If each leaf has four or more leaflets, it's poison sumac. Don't touch the leaves or the berries of these plants. Don't eat any berry unless you are absolutely, positively sure it is safe for human consumption. (Most plant books contain photographs of poisonous varieties.)

*Berries, exotic cones, and pods combine to achieve stunning results in this elegant holiday wreath.*

# Holiday Wreath

## WHAT YOU NEED

50 acorns without caps or 3 bunches of artificial grapes

2 dried poppy seed heads

12-inch-diameter grapevine wreath base

3 begun fruit pods

4 rose cones

2 spider cones

4 badam fruit pods

4 menzeii cones

12 stems of dried bay leaves, 6 inches long

7 stems of dried dusty miller, 6 inches long

1 small bunch of ornamental grass, 4 inches long

Hot-glue gun and glue sticks

Acrylic spray paints in red, black, and gold metallic

Clear acrylic spray

Spool of fine-gauge floral wire

Wire cutters

Floral picks

Floral tape

1 small handful of white, unspun wool

24 inches of gold-trimmed red velvet wired ribbon, 3 inches wide

Scissors

## WHAT YOU DO

*1* If you are using acorns, hot-glue them onto the base. Set aside 15 acorns and spray the remaining acorns with red acrylic paint. Standing about 2 feet away, mist the red acorns with black paint to make them more of a cherry color. Then, using the gold paint, spray the set-aside acorns or 15 of the artificial grapes gold. Lightly spray one-quarter of the pods, cones, and poppy seed heads with the gold paint. When they are dry, spray some of the painted acorns with clear acrylic and mist some of them with gold paint. If you are using artificial grapes, spray them with clear acrylic. Let all the materials dry.

*2* In a symmetrical pattern around the wreath base, hot-glue the pods and cones to the base in this order: begun fruit pods, rose cones, spider cones, badam fruit pods, and menzeii cones, being sure to place some of each kind on the inner and outer rims and on the front of the wreath.

*3* Hot-glue small bunches of the cherry-colored acorns or clear-glossed grapes to fill in some of the spaces around the base and at the top center. Hot-glue the bay leaf stems to the base, inserting them behind the cones and pods. Hot-glue the poppy seed heads and the gold acorns to the base, making sure to hot-glue some to the apex of the badam or inside the begun fruit pods.

*4* Wire the seven stems of dusty miller to floral picks and then wrap the stems with floral tape. Pick them into the top center of the wreath and halfway down the wreath behind the acorns on both sides—on the inner and outer rims and at the bottom of the wreath.

5 Hot-glue little bits of wool in an even fashion around the wreath.

6 Make a full, two-loop bow with the wired ribbon; cut sparrow's tails on both ends (see "Two-Loop Bow" on page 52), and hot-glue the bow to the top of the wreath. Then put a dab of hot glue on the ends of the fragile ornamental grass and insert the grass behind the pods and cones.

# Bittersweet Wreath

## WHAT YOU NEED

6 to 8 lengths of oriental bittersweet vine, full of berries (they ripen in the fall), 6 feet long

1 wasp nest

2 artificial or dead wasps or other insects

Hot-glue gun and glue sticks

## WHAT YOU DO

1 Use six to eight 6-foot lengths of the vine or the equivalent in shorter or longer pieces. It is best to work with the vine as soon as possible after you cut it because it is more pliable then and the berries, which grow only on the female plants, stay on the vine more securely. Don't trim any of the offshoot tendrils because they hold most of the berries and add a lot of texture and interest to the completed wreath.

*Made from oriental bittersweet, this wreath seems to glow in the same autumn sunlight that ripens its brilliant orange berries.*

2 Strip off all the leaves, then twist and intertwine the vine into a 16-inch circle. Start with a single length of vine and add one piece at a time until all of the vine pieces are incorporated. Use the crooked vines to your advantage; don't try to tame them.

3 Hot-glue the wasp nest where it looks most interesting. Hot-glue the wasps or other insects on or near the nest to give your wreath a true nature look—without the bite!

# BOWS

A perfectly placed bow can tie together all the elements of a crafted piece and can give it a special personality. An organdy bow with long ribbon tails can be the main attraction of a wreath, such as the "Victorian Wreath" on page 90. A wired ribbon can be an integral part of the design, as in the "Victorian Twig Swag" on page 204. Or a simple raffia bow can be treated as one more material, as in the "Kitchen Herb Swag" on page 202.

Once you have learned the basics of making a bow, the hard part will be choosing from among the many different types of ribbon that are available. A visit to a well-stocked fabric store, craft-supply store, Christmas shop, or florist will reveal a dazzling array of ribbon. You may be wooed by the cotton tapestry, the sheers in floral prints or metallic gold, or the dressy organdy. The best way to learn about fabric characteristics is to purchase 2 to 3 yards of each ribbon and to practice making bows. In general, you'll want to practice on inexpensive ribbon. But for your projects, try to use high-quality ribbon since it will give your finished piece a much more polished look. The "Bow Options" chart on page 48 lists the main types of ribbon and describes advantages and drawbacks of each.

## Attaching Bows

A bow is usually hot-glued or wired to a base, but it can also be wired onto a floral pick and then picked into the base. A long length of ribbon can be secured to the base with straight pins. Some ribbon, such as wired ribbon, can be twisted and curled around the base and then held in place with small dabs of hot glue.

A bow or ribbon can be the first or the last material to be attached. If you are working with fragile, dried flowers, you may want to attach the bow before you attach all your flowers so that you don't disturb them. If you secure the bow early on, you may decide to decorate it with natural materials, too. Be careful not to drip hot glue on the visible part of the ribbon.

# BOW OPTIONS

## Cellophane

*Advantages* • Available in a wide range of bright colors; adds holiday spirit to projects; easy to work with.

*Drawbacks* • Bright, metallic colors have limited design applications.

## Cotton

*Advantages* • Available in a wide range of colors, prints, and widths; good for beginners because creases can be ironed out and ribbon reused; printed ribbons are a great option for matching room decor; inexpensive and good material for practice.

*Drawbacks* • Fabric can be stiff; takes some practice to make a well-proportioned bow.

## Lace

*Advantages* • Available in several widths; perfect for weddings, births, and other special occasions; for the highest quality appearance, select cotton lace.

*Drawbacks* • Is not very stiff and the bow loops may not hold their shape very well, but it can be dipped in liquid fabric stiffener before tying the bow.

## Paper

*Advantages* • Available in a wide range of colors and widths; good for beginners; ties easily into simple bows and can be reshaped and reused.

*Drawbacks* • Bows tend to be casual, not dressy; buy ribbon that comes already unraveled, because twisted paper ribbon, though inexpensive, is time-consuming to unravel.

## Raffia

*Advantages* • Available in different widths; adds a natural touch to projects; is easy to work with; can be easily dyed to match materials and room settings.

*Drawbacks* • Natural look may limit design applications.

## Satin

*Advantages* • Available in a wide range of colors and widths; can be hot-glued to straw and polystyrene bases to give them a more attractive appearance; inexpensive and good material for practice.

*Drawbacks* • Fabric is slippery and can be a challenge to crafters just learning to tie bows.

## Velvet

*Advantages* • Available in a wide range of colors and widths; adds a formal and elegant look; works well on a grand scale.

*Drawbacks* • Has limited design applications because it is so dressy; is easily crushed and not reusable; can be expensive.

## Wired (also known as French ribbon)

*Advantages* • Wrong side is lined with a row of thin-gauge wire on both edges; available in a wide range of colors, including variegated hues, prints, and widths; easy to work with; can be shaped and reshaped again and again.

*Drawbacks* • Can be expensive.

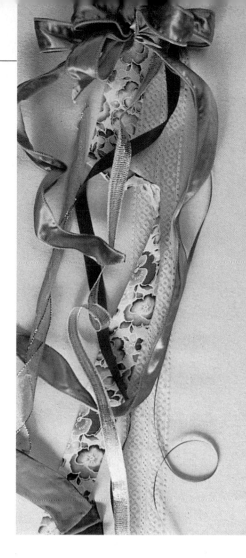

# Nine-Loop Bow

## WHAT YOU NEED

3 yards of ribbon

6 inches of thin-gauge floral wire wrapped in floral tape

Scissors

*With this one approach, you can make a 5-loop or a 15-loop bow.*

## WHAT YOU DO

*1* Pinch the ribbon between your thumb and index finger, 4½ inches away from the end of the ribbon and twist. Keep the right side of the ribbon facing you at all times.

*2* Make a loop two-thirds the length of the streamer or tail (about 2¾ inches), put it behind the tail, pinch, and twist.

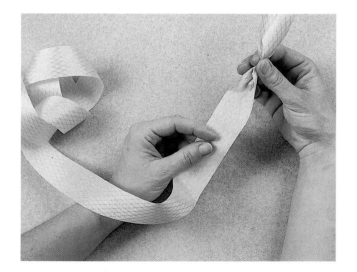

3 Make a second loop of the same length as the first, put it behind the tail, pinch it, and twist it so that the right side is again facing you. Repeat this process six more times so that you wind up with four loops on top and four on the bottom. If you want a dome-shaped bow, make loops four through eight each slightly larger than the one before it.

4 For the ninth loop—the center loop—make a loop the size of the first loop, and pinch and twist it so that the right side is facing you. Pull the taped floral wire through the center loop; wrap the wire around the center of all the loops, pull it tight, and twist it. To fluff the bow, tug and twist each loop; you can also fluff the loops by ironing them with a warm curling iron.

5 To finish the bow, cut the other end of the ribbon so that you have a second 4½-inch-long tail. Cut the two tails either on the diagonal or with a V-shaped cut (or sparrow's tail).

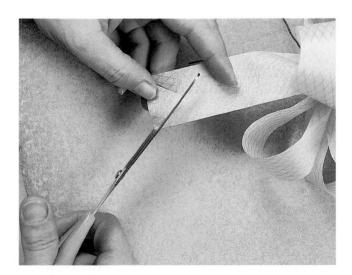

# Two-Loop Bow

## WHAT YOU NEED

2 yards of ribbon

Scissors

## WHAT YOU DO

*1* Make a 4½-inch center loop, leaving a 1-foot-long tail, and pinch and twist the ribbon, keeping the right side facing you.

*2* Wrap a second loop around your hand and twist it gently so that the right side of the ribbon remains facing you.

*3* Fold the ribbon to make the third loop and pull it through the center loop; pull the loops until a tight knot is formed.

*4* Adjust the loops and the tails and fluff the bow. Cut the other end of the ribbon so you have a second 1-foot-long tail. Cut the two tails either on the diagonal or with a V-shaped cut (or sparrow's tail).

# CONES, PODS & NUTS

# C

Nothing adds more drama and texture to a nature project than cones, pods, and nuts. While they are not as showy as flowers nor as fragrant as herbs, their distinctive shapes and textures make them handsome additions to any craft project (see "Holiday Wreath" on page 44). Best of all, cones and pods are abundant along roadsides, in fields, and right in your own backyard. Gather them by the bagful and use different types and sizes together in the same project. Or just use one material, such as cones, for beautiful results.

## Preparing Cones, Pods, and Nuts For Use

Before using cones, pods, and nuts they must be heated to kill any little creatures (insect eggs or larvae) in residence. This is a simple process. Spread them in a single layer on a baking sheet and bake them in a 200°F oven for 25 minutes, or you can use a microwave oven.

Microwaving offers the additional benefit of opening up the petals of the cones, which will make them easier to wire. To microwave cones, place four or five of them into a paper bag and heat them on 50 percent power for eight to ten minutes. If the cone petals are not as open as you'd like, heat them in three-minute intervals until the petals open.

To prepare pods or nuts for microwaving, place 7 to 12 of them into a brown bag and heat them for eight to ten minutes at 50 percent power to kill any larvae and to open up any contracted pods.

## Sections or Parts of Cones

Many times a craft project calls for sections or parts of cones or pods, such as cone flowers—traditional modifications of whole cones. To make a cone flower, simply cut between two layers of petals, using heavy scissors or pruning shears. Most crafters leave four to eight layers of petals on their cone flowers, which can then be wired or glued onto the project.

Some pods are actually more interesting on the inside than the outside. You can use a sharp serrated knife to slice dried pods into crosswise or lengthwise portions. Pods are best sliced before baking, as baking may make them a bit more brittle.

Some of the best cones for projects are listed on page 54. To get cones and pods that are not indigenous to your area of the country, try ordering them from some of the sources listed in the "Supply Sources" on page 254. If you plan on collecting cones, pods, and nuts yourself, remember to gather them after they are fully mature but before they have begun to rot.

## How to Attach Cones, Pods, and Nuts

You can attach these items in a number of ways. Small cones, pods, and nuts can simply be hot-glued onto a base. If the base is polystyrene, use cool-melt glue so that you don't melt it. If you plan to hot-glue cones, pods, and nuts to a flat surface, such as a piece of wood, first cover the surface with a sturdy fabric, like cotton muslin; then you can hot-glue your materials to the fabric.

You can attach cones by wiring them as follows: Slip a length of fine-gauge floral wire around the bottom of the cone between two layers of cone petals and fold the wire in half. Twist the wire ends together until they are tightly woven right up against the bottom of the cone. Wrap this wire around the wreath base or through a grapevine strand—or around whatever you are attaching the cone to—and twist again (see Figure 1). Extremely heavy cones may need to be reinforced with several dabs of hot glue. If the cone is small and fragile, you can simply loop the end of the wire around the bottom of the cone and leave a single long wire stem to wrap around or insert into the base (see Figure 2). For some projects, such as the "S-Curve Cone Centerpiece" on page 55, you will need to drill through the stem end of a cone, pod, or nut with a ⅛-inch drill bit and slip the wire through the hole.

Small seedpods and seed heads can also be attached to bases with floral picks. Hot-glue the flat end of the pick to the material and then insert the tapered end into the base.

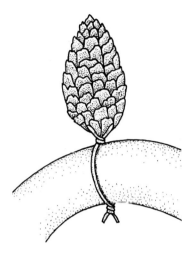

*Figure 1*

*Figure 2*

# Cones for Craft Projects

- Arborvitae
- Australian pine
- Blue spruce
- Cedar
- Cypress
- Fir
- Hemlock
- Juniper
- Longleaf pine
- Norway spruce
- Pinyon pine
- Red pine
- Redwood
- Scotch pine
- Sequoia
- Sugar pine
- Virginia pine
- White pine
- White spruce

# Pods for Craft Projects

- Badam fruit
- Begun fruit
- Daylily
- Eucalyptus
- Hare's-tail grass
- Honey locust
- Jack fruit
- Lotus
- Magnolia
- Milkweed
- Palm
- Poppy
- Pussy willow
- Scotch broom
- Sweet gum
- Teasel
- Wisteria
- Yucca

# Nuts for Crafts Projects

- Acorn
- Chestnut
- Hazelnut
- Hickory nut
- Pecan
- Walnut

To give nuts a dressier look, spray paint them gold. For a gold-dusting effect, stand about 2 feet away from the nuts and spray them with short, quick bursts of paint, moving your hand constantly to give an even dusting. You can use this dusting technique on cones and pods, too, (see "Woodland Fireplace Screen" on page 56).

To create a fruitlike appearance, spray the nuts with red paint; when dry, spray them with a high-gloss acrylic. Or, before applying the layer of gloss, stand back 2 feet and spray the nuts very lightly with black paint: this will give them a cherry-red color.

# S-Curve Cone Centerpiece

*This fanciful curved centerpiece is the perfect complement to any holiday dinner or special occasion.*

## What You Need

24 petals from longleaf pinecones

4 large longleaf pinecones

8 red-spruce cones

28 inches of heavy-gauge wire

Brown floral tape

Electric drill with ⅛-inch drill bit

32 pieces of medium-gauge wire, 6 inches long

4 pieces of medium-gauge wire, 9 inches long

Wire cutters

Clear varnish spray

2 votive candles (optional)

## What You Do

1 Twist the heavy-gauge wire into an S shape and completely wrap it with brown floral tape.

2 Drill small holes in the bases of the 24 petals from the longleaf pinecones.

3 Wrap twenty-four 6-inch-long pieces of medium-gauge wire with brown floral tape. Thread one wire through each petal and twist, leaving about a 4-inch length for a stem.

4 Wrap the four pieces of 9-inch-long medium-gauge wire with brown floral tape. Cut the four longleaf pinecones to make flowers (see "Sections or Parts of Cones" on page 53). Wrap the wire around the bottom petals and twist. Leave about 5 inches of wire for a stem.

55

5 Wrap each of the remaining 6-inch-long medium-gauge wire pieces with brown floral tape and wrap each piece around a red-spruce cone as in Step 4 on page 55, leaving a 4-inch stem.

6 Using the wire stems to attach the cones, place the large cone flowers onto the S shape, following the photograph on page 55. In the same manner, attach the red-spruce cones and cone petals.

7 Rewrap the entire S-shaped base with brown floral tape until all the wires are covered and smooth. Spray the entire centerpiece with clear varnish and allow it to dry. Add votive candles to match your decor, if desired.

# Woodland Fireplace Screen

## WHAT YOU NEED

500 to 600 cones and pods of assorted types and sizes

100 acorns, chestnuts, locust burrs, peach pits, and other interesting hulls and nuts

20 clusters of dried pepperberries or dried flowers

Jigsaw with a plywood blade

1 piece of plywood, ¼ inch thick, large enough to fit the dimensions of your fireplace opening (The screen shown in the photo on the opposite page measures 24 × 36 inches.)

Yardstick

Pencil

36 inches of string or flexible tubing

3 large shelf brackets and accompanying screws

Electric drill with bit size one size smaller than the screws for the shelf brackets

Screwdriver

3 yards of cotton muslin

Scissors

Hammer

Small tacks

Pruning shears

White craft glue

Clear varnish spray

Metallic gold spray paint (optional)

## WHAT YOU DO

1 Using the jigsaw, cut the plywood to size. Use the pencil and yardstick to measure and mark the dimensions on the wood. Use the pencil and the string or the flexible tubing to outline a nice arc connecting your dimensions. When you are satisfied with the arc, draw it in pencil and cut out the fan-shaped screen with a jigsaw.

2 To attach the shelf brackets, drill holes in the bottom of the wood on the back of the fan, making sure not to drill all the way through the wood. Then, place the brackets on the wood, aligning the holes for the screws with the holes in the wood. Use the screwdriver to screw the brackets to the wood. If you attach the brackets at this stage, you will be completing Steps 4 through 7 with the fan in an upright position. You can choose to add the brackets after completing Step 7; to do so, ask a friend to hold the screen upright while you attach the brackets.

3 Because the pinecones will not adhere well to the smooth surface of the plywood, you need to cover the plywood with fabric. Using the scissors, cut the muslin to fit the front of the fan, stretch it tightly, and tack it securely to the back side of the wood. Cut off any excess fabric. On the front side of the fan, randomly hammer tacks into the wood, peppering the fabric with tacks so it will not be able to pull away from the wood.

4 You are now ready to glue on the natural materials. Assess your collection of cones. You may want to cut some of the very tall cones to create cone flowers (see "Sections or Parts of Cones" on page 53). Before you start to glue, here are a few design guidelines to help you. (a) Glue the largest pinecones in the middle of the fan; this placement should not be symmetrical but should appear random. (b) Because the appeal of this project depends on the texture created by the cones, it is a good practice to vary their height by placing short cones near taller ones. This does not mean you should glue a 1-inch hemlock cone next to a 1 foot sugar-pine cone, but rather that you can place a 4- to 5-inch Douglas-fir cone next to a 9-inch longleaf pinecone. (c) Always work the height of the cones up and down slightly. (d) The more varieties of cones you have to work with, the better!

5 When you have completely covered the fan with cones, it is time to look for holes in your design. If you can see the fabric, glue on a peach pit or acorn to provide coverage and add visual interest. Take your time; a large fan will take a minimum of five to six hours to completely cover with materials. Make sure all the edges of the design area are covered with stable cones that are not likely to break.

6 Take your fan outdoors. Spray first with a clear varnish and let dry (this will take about two hours). If you want to gild your fan, spray it now with the metallic gold paint. If you don't want a heavy layer of gold, stand about 2 feet away from the fan, and spray in short, quick puffs of paint, constantly moving the can around the fan. This technique will give the appearance of gold dusting and will permit some of the natural tones of the cones to show through. If you are unsure how to achieve this effect, practice on a piece of newspaper first.

7 Finish the fan by gluing on the color accents, in this case, red pepperberries. These accents should match your decor, and may be as simple as dried statice. Just a few sprigs of flowers or a cluster of berries tucked here and there is enough to pick up the colors in a room. If the fan needs cleaning, use a vacuum cleaner; after a few years, you may want to respray it with varnish. Store the fan away from excessive heat.

*Ideal for camouflaging unsightly ashes and charred logs, this impressive fireplace screen is a great way to make use of all those cones, pods, and nuts you collect on your walks through the woods.*

# Nut, Pod & Berry Wreath

*Pepperberries and gold cording add a hint of glamour to this delightful and nutty mix of natural materials.*

## WHAT YOU NEED

12 dried Siberian iris pods

50 hazelnuts

20 Brazil nuts

4 almonds

2 pecans

1 piece of sheet moss, 15 inches square (available at craft-supply and hobby stores)

15 sprigs of dried pink pepperberries

10-inch-diameter polystyrene wreath base

6 inches of heavy-gauge floral wire

Gold acrylic spray paint

Cool-melt glue gun and glue sticks

Pencil

15 inches of braided cording

## WHAT YOU DO

*1* With the heavy-gauge wire, fashion a hanger (see "Hangers" on page 118) and attach it to the polystyrene wreath base. Spray the iris pods gold and set them aside to dry.

*2* Cool-glue all of the nuts onto the polystyrene base, generously covering the front of the wreath, with a smaller number on the inner and outer rims. Cool-glue some nuts on top of other nuts. Vary the angles of the nuts to create a pleasing arrangement.

*3* Squirt a small amount of cool-melt glue into the spaces between the nuts.

With a pencil, poke little bits of sheet moss onto the glue. When all the gaps are filled with moss, cool-glue larger pieces of moss to completely cover the rest of the base, including the inner and outer rims and the back.

*4* Cool-glue the sprigs of pepperberries all over the wreath. Then cool-glue the gold iris pods on the inner and outer rims of the wreath.

*5* Cool-glue the cording to the left-hand side of the wreath, being sure to fasten it at all the places where it loops and curves.

*Intricate but simple-to-make hemlock spheres look natural and attractive hanging on a Christmas tree or in a doorway.*

# Hemlock Kissing Balls

## WHAT YOU NEED (for each ball)

30 hemlock cones, gathered as soon as possible after they mature

1-inch-diameter polystyrene ball

Black shoe polish

30 pieces of fine-gauge wire, 5 inches long

Wire cutters

White glue

6 inches of medium-gauge wire

Clear varnish spray

## WHAT YOU DO

1 Cover the polystyrene ball with black shoe polish and allow it to dry.

2 Using the 5-inch lengths of fine-gauge wire, wrap the bottom petals of each hemlock cone with a piece of wire, twist the ends together, and snip the wire with the wire cutters to leave a ¾-inch-long stem.

3 Dip the ends of the wire stems into white glue and stick the wired cones into the polystyrene ball. Cover the entire ball with cones. Allow the glue to dry.

4 Spray the ball with clear acrylic varnish and allow it to dry. Attach the medium-gauge wire for a hanger (see "Hangers" on page 118).

# CORNHUSKS

Cornhusk crafting surely must be the quintessential nature craft—humble in origin, centuries old, and downright fun to learn.

Most craft-supply stores sell dried cornhusks in 4-ounce packages, but you'll also find fresh husks right on the sweet corn in your local grocery store and, if you live in a rural area, on the corn in the fields. To cure your own green husks, strip them gently from the ears of corn and spread them out on newspapers to dry.

The dried husks are brittle, so before you can work with them you'll need to soak them for about 15 minutes in a bucket or pan filled with hot water. If you have trouble separating tightly bundled commercial husks, place the entire bundle in warm water until the husks are soft enough to peel apart. Once they're wet, the husks can be kept in the refrigerator for up to two weeks and can be frozen indefinitely. To keep the husks damp as you work, wrap them in a moistened towel.

Both natural-colored and dyed husks are available at craft-supply stores, but if you'd like to extend your color choices, you can do your own dyeing. Just mix fabric dye according to the instructions on the dye package and soak the husks in the dye bath until they're the desired shade. (An overnight soaking may be necessary for deep shades.) One tip: When you work with dyed husks, be sure they're damp rather than dripping wet, or the dye may bleed.

Note that cornhusks are textured, with a grain that runs along their length. Always cut and roll the husks so that the grain runs from one end of the piece you are making to the other.

To make the projects that follow, soak your cornhusks and assemble your materials before you start.

*Decorative cornhusk dolls only look complicated. Follow the instructions for the "Basic Cornhusk Doll" on page 62 to create one of the attractive medium-size dolls shown here.*

# Basic Cornhusk Doll

## WHAT YOU NEED

2 ounces of natural-colored cornhusks

½ ounce of green-colored cornhusks

½ ounce of red-colored cornhusks

1 tuft of dried corn silk, about ½ × ¾ × 4 inches

2 or 3 tiny sprigs of dried blooms

3 inches of heavy-gauge floral wire

Scissors

1-inch-diameter, rigid polystyrene ball

8 pieces of fine-gauge floral wire, 4 inches long

8 inches of medium-gauge floral wire

Wire cutters

2 or 3 sheets of white paper

White craft glue

Hot-glue gun and glue sticks

## WHAT YOU DO

*1* Bend over ½ inch of the 3-inch-long heavy-gauge wire to form a small hook. Cut a 2 × 4-inch piece of the natural-colored cornhusk, gather it in the center, and catch the gather in the wire hook. Push the other end of the wire through the center of the polystyrene ball and pull the wire all the way through the ball, until the hook is seated firmly in the upper portion of the ball (see Figure 1). Spread the husk to cover the ball and twist a piece of the fine-gauge wire around the husk, just beneath the head you've created (see Figure 2). Use the wire cutters to trim the ends of the wire.

*2* To make the arms, place the 8-inch-long piece of medium-gauge wire on one long edge of an 8-inch-long piece of natural-colored cornhusk and roll the husk tightly around the wire to form a cylinder. Tie the center of the cylinder with a piece of the fine-gauge wire and trim the cylinder ends to make a 7½-inch-long arm piece (see Figure 3).

*3* To make the sleeves that cover each arm, gather a 3 × 3½-inch piece of husk around one arm, about ½ inch from its end, and twist a piece of the fine-gauge wire around it to fasten it in place. Then turn this husk inside out, folding it back toward the center of the cylinder. Use a piece of fine-gauge wire to tie down the folded sleeve near the center of the arm piece (see Figure 4). Repeat this process to form another sleeve at the other end of the cylinder.

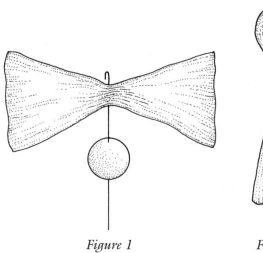

*Figure 1*

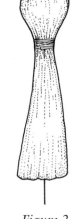

*Figure 2*

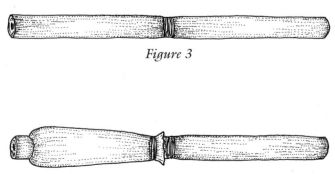

*Figure 3*

*Figure 4*

*4* Position the arm piece underneath the head and between the pieces of husk that form the neck. Place a piece of the fine-gauge wire underneath the arm piece and tie the arm piece in place (see Figure 5). Cut two pieces of the natural-colored husk for the bodice, each about 1½ × 5 inches. Hide the long, raw edges of each piece by folding them toward the center of each piece. Place the center of each strip on a shoulder and bring the ends down the front and back, crossing them at the waist (see Figure 6).

*5* To make the apron straps that rest over the bodice, start with two ¾ × 5-inch strips of the green husk, folding them to hide any raw edges. Drape these over the shoulders. Then twist a piece of the fine-gauge wire around the waist to secure the bodice and straps to the torso.

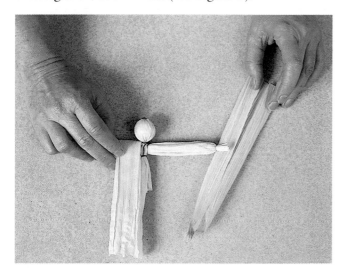

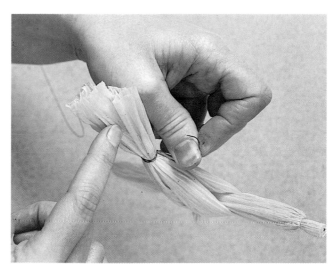

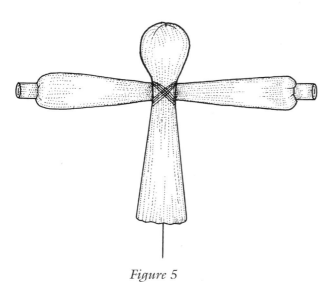

*Figure 5*

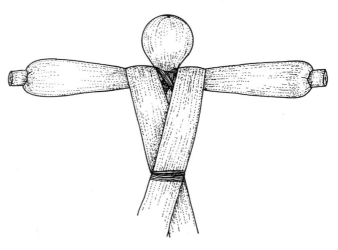

*Figure 6*

6 To make the skirt, bend the arms up out of your way. Place four to six of the nicest-looking green husks evenly around the chest and head, gathering them into soft folds as you work and overlapping the waist wire by about ½ inch. (Note that the photo shows a skirt being made with natural-colored husks; you may use husks of any color.) Wrap a piece of the fine-gauge wire tightly around the doll's waist.

7 Gently fold the husks down into position, shaping them as you turn them right side out (see Figure 7 on the opposite page). Trim the bottom of the skirt to make it even. To make the apron, cut a piece of the red husk about 1 inch longer than the skirt. Use a small strip of red husk—or natural-colored husk, if you prefer—to tie the apron piece around the waist so that its bottom edge is slightly above the bottom of the skirt.

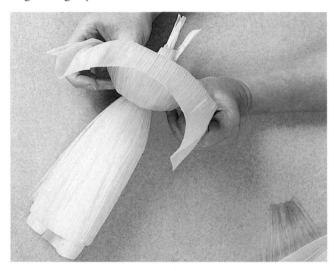

## Pilgrim Doll

### ADDITIONAL MATERIALS

Substitute 1 ounce of black-colored cornhusks for the red and the green cornhusks in the "Basic Cornhusk Doll" on page 62.

### WHAT YOU DO

1 Following the instructions for the "Basic Cornhusk Doll," use the natural-colored husks to make the arms, head, hat, and apron. Use black husks for the sleeves, bodice, and skirt. (Omit the apron straps.)

2 Cut a thin piece of the natural-colored husk to form a collar around the doll's neck. Trim the collar as needed and hot-glue it to her shoulders, front, and back.

*8* While the arms are still damp, reposition them as desired. Stuff the skirts with white paper so that they'll hold their shape as they dry. Allow the doll to dry for about three days.

*9* When the doll is completely dry, cover the top and back of the head with white craft glue and wrap it with the corn silk. Be sure to trim away those split ends! To make the hat, first cut a 5-inch square of the red husk. Fold one edge over about ½ inch to form a smooth front edge. Hot-glue the hat to the top of the doll's head. Then pinch the back portion of the hat into a fold behind the back of her head and apply hot glue to secure (see Figure 8). Tie a thin piece of the red husk around the doll's neck, making a bow under her chin.

*10* Hot-glue the tiny sprigs of dried blooms to one of the doll's hands.

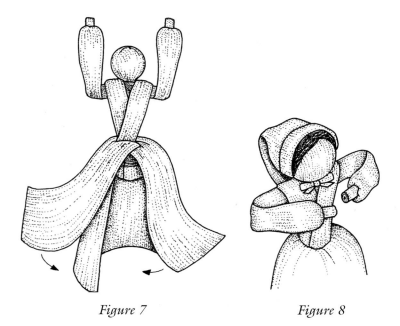

*Figure 7*      *Figure 8*

# Broom

To make a broom for any cornhusk doll, wrap a 1½ × 3-inch piece of natural-colored husk around a craft pick, using a short length of heavy thread to tie it in place. Then tie the pick to the doll's hand with a short length of string.

# Cornhusk Santa

## ADDITIONAL MATERIALS

Red fabric dye

Substitute 3 ounces of natural-colored cornhusks for all of the husks in the "Basic Cornhusk Doll" on page 62

White fleece fabric

4 inches of fine-gauge floral wire

Straight pin

## WHAT YOU DO

*1* Following the instructions on the dye package, prepare the dye double strength. Soak about three-fourths of the husks in the bath until they're the desired shade of red. Leave the remaining husks undyed.

*2* Assemble the "Basic Cornhusk Doll" but use red husks to make all of the parts, except for the natural-colored head and arms. (Don't make the hat yet.)

*3* When the doll is completely dry, glue small pieces of the white fleece onto Santa's skirt and around the ends of his sleeves, as shown in the photograph.

*4* To make the beard-and-hair piece, gather two 9-inch-long pieces of natural-colored husk in the center and wrap them with the piece of fine-gauge wire. Using the straight pin, shred the cornhusks on one side of the wire to form the beard. Secure the beard-and-hair piece to the top of the head by wrapping and hot-gluing the unshredded section around the head to form hair.

*5* Shred a 2-inch-long piece of natural-colored husk to make Santa's moustache and hot-glue it to the beard.

*6* To make the hat, which is longer than the hat on the basic cornhusk doll, use a 5-inch-square piece of red husk. Turn one 5-inch edge of the husk back on itself to form a smooth front edge and hot-glue the hat to the head. When the glue is dry, hot-glue a fold into the flowing back portion of the hat (see Figure 8 on page 65).

*7* Roll a 1½-inch square of red husk into a loose tube to form Santa's list. Tie it with a small strand of husk and hot-glue it to Santa's hand, just below his fleece cuff.

# Cornhusk Bookmarks

## WHAT YOU NEED (for 1 bookmark)

½ ounce of natural-colored cornhusks

½ ounce of dyed cornhusks, any color

1 tuft of dried corn silk, 2 inches long

Scissors

No. 20 crochet thread

White craft glue

Old magazine or catalog

Heavy object, such as a large book

Fine-tipped colored pens

## WHAT YOU DO

*1* Cut a 1½ × 3-inch strip of natural-colored husk and fold it in half to make a square. Then fold the folded edge down about ½ inch. Starting at one short edge, roll the folded husk into a tube, with the fold on the outer surface (see Figure 1 on page 68). The thicker portion will serve as the head of the bookmark, and the thinner portion will form the neck. Use the crochet thread to tie the roll together just below the head.

*2* Cut a 1 × 4½-inch strip of natural-colored husk. Drape the strip over the head, with about 3½ inches of husk covering the face and about 1 inch behind the head. Spread the front of this husk to cover the front of the head and fasten it by tying thread around the neck (see Figure 2 on page 68). Split the front portion of the husk into two long strips, stopping the split just under the tie at the neck.

*3* To form the arms, twist each strip into a very tight roll and then double each roll back on itself to form a 1-inch-long arm; about ½ inch of roll will be left at the end (see Figure 3 on page 68). Press the ½-inch portion of each arm down the back

of the torso and use the thread to fasten them below the neck.

*4* Wrapping the arms with dyed husk is easier than it looks; it's done bandage style. Cut a ⅝ × 4¾-inch strip of husk. Place one end at an angle across the front of the torso piece. While holding that end in place, bring the husk up and over one shoulder and wrap it around the arm two or three times, leaving ⅛ inch of exposed arm to represent a hand. Draw the husk around the back of the torso, under the other arm,

*You'll never lose your place when it's held by a charming cornhusk bookmark.*

67

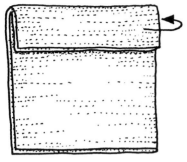

*Figure 1*

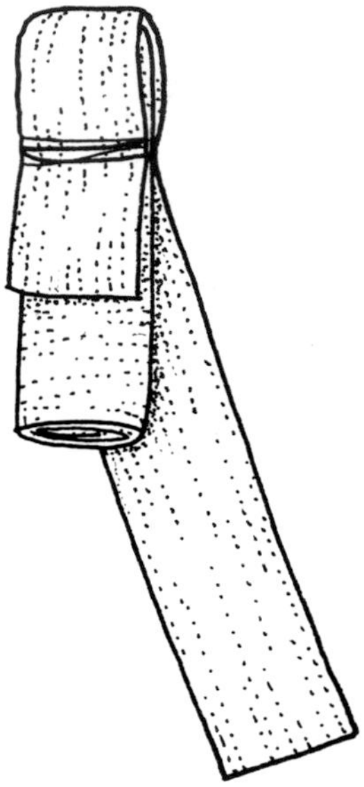

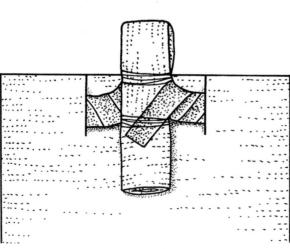

*Figure 2*

and wrap the other arm in the same manner. Finally, bring the loose end of the husk straight down the torso's back (see Figure 4). Then secure both husk ends—one in front and one in back—by tying a piece of the thread around the waist.

5 To make the skirt, start with a 4 × 7-inch dyed husk. At one end of the husk, cut two ½-inch-deep slits, each about

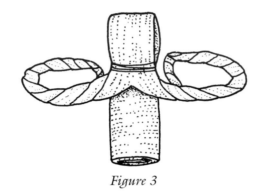

*Figure 3*

*Figure 4*

½ inch in from the long edges. Lay the torso face down on the strip, lining up its neck with the edge between the slits. Slip the arms through the slits (see Figure 5) and pull the husk back to overlap behind the neck. Tie the dress together, first with thread and then with ⅛-inch-wide strips of husk, at the waist and at the neck, trimming the ends at each knot.

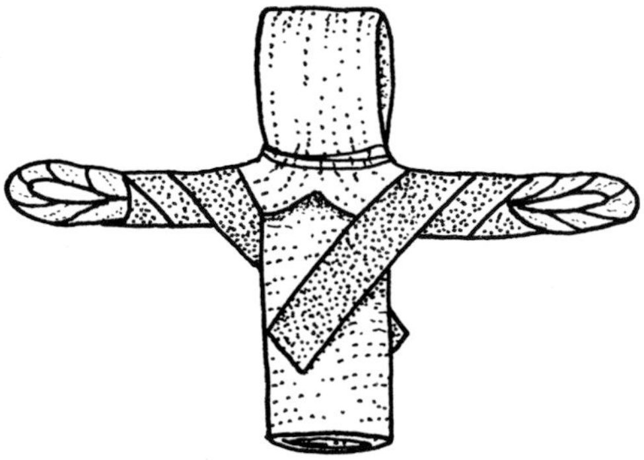

6 To make the hair, drape a 2-inch-long bundle of corn silk over the head so that one end covers the face and the other spreads down the back. About ⅛ inch down from the top of the head, tie a piece of the thread around the hair and head to fasten the hair in place. Then pull the silk that rests in front over the head to cover the thread (see Figure 6). Braid or twist the silks, using a tiny amount of craft glue to keep them from unraveling. Tie the braid at its base, first with the thread and then with a narrow piece of husk.

7 To press the skirt flat as the bookmark dries, slip it inside an old magazine or catalog and place a heavy object on top. (Be careful not to use printed matter that will release dyes or inks onto the damp cornhusks.)

8 When the bookmark has dried completely, use colored pens to draw on the face.

*Figure 5*

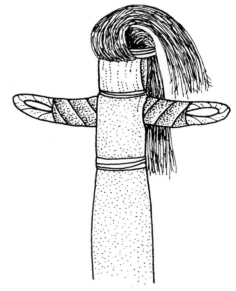

*Figure 6*

# Cornhusk Dogwoods

*Who says that you can't create nature crafts if you live in the city? A quick trip to your local grocery store and craft shop will yield all you need to bring spring blossoms into your home.*

## WHAT YOU NEED (for 1 flower)

1 or 2 natural-colored cornhusks

1 light green-colored cornhusk

Tracing paper

Pencil

Scissors

18 inches of heavy-gauge floral wire

4½ inches of medium-gauge floral wire

11 inches of medium-gauge floral wire

Wire cutters

Straight pin

Pliers

3 inches of masking tape

Green floral tape

Light red or pink fingernail polish

# D DRYING

Working with fresh-cut floral materials is wonderfully satisfying. But unless you're a florist or live in the tropics, you'll find that dried materials offer at least two advantages over fresh-cut: They last indefinitely, and they are available year-round. Many dried materials, including everlastings, fruits, herbs, and flowers, are available from craft-supply stores, florists, and mail-order companies, which often sell standard dried blooms in bunches of bundled stems. (See "Supply Sources" on page 254.)

While commercially dried materials are readily available, they are somewhat limited in range and can be quite expensive. Fortunately, drying your own plant materials at home is remarkably easy. Even those of you who don't own gardens will find that a brief trip to the grocery store or a midsummer stroll along your favorite country lane will yield hundreds of suitable plant materials.

Perhaps the single disadvantage to drying your own floral materials is that it can be addictive. Every corner of your home will soon be filled with bundles of fragrant, colorful plants, so give your family fair warning!

## Expectations and Reality

Novice crafters may be disappointed by the results of their first experiments with drying. For the sake of your spirits, keep in mind that bloom and foliage colors often change as plants lose moisture; don't expect dried materials to be the same colors as fresh ones. Unless you're working with true everlastings, such as strawflowers, you'll quickly realize that the palette offered by dried materials will take a bit of experience to determine in advance. White blooms, for example, often fade to an off-white or beige color, and the stunning deep reds of some roses may change to equally attractive but very different red-blacks.

Remember, too, that no matter which drying method you use or how careful you are, many factors—some more controllable than others—will come into play, among them the humidity of your environment, the stage at which the materials are harvested, and the varieties of flowers or herbs that you are drying. We certainly don't mean to dampen your enthusiasm, but even experienced nature crafters know that although drying plant materials is tremendously rewarding, the results aren't always consistent.

To ease the learning process, keep a notebook and record in it the results of every foray you make into the world of drying. As you accumulate information in that notebook, by all means use it to adapt the general instructions provided in this chapter. The "Plants for Drying" chart on page 80 should also help you move toward expertise!

## Harvesting

Whether you're working in your own garden or plan to collect wild plant materials, take along a large basket and sharp pruning shears. Protect your hands by wearing gloves and your skin by wearing sunblock lotion and a wide-brimmed hat. Always pick fresh plant materials on a warm, sunny day after the morning dew has evaporated; plants that are moist when harvested are likely to develop molds as they dry, and the blooms may turn brown as well. Avoid late-afternoon harvesting, however, as the hot sun may cause blooms to wilt.

Select only the healthiest plants; blemishes on leaves and blooms will only be accentuated by drying. To harvest seed heads and blooms, cut the stems between 2 and 12 inches long (the longer, the better). Because many materials shrink as they dry—some by more than 50 percent—collect more than you think you'll need. Place the cut materials in your basket, alternating the direction in which you set the blossom ends so that the petals and the leaves won't be crushed. Plan on dry-

ing your harvest as soon as possible. The longer you wait, the less pleasing the results will be.

If you're harvesting materials from the wild, pay close attention to two firm rules: Know what you're harvesting so that you can avoid collecting endangered species and never take more than one-third of any type of plant. The patch of wild grasses that you pass on your daily walks may call out to the craft designer in you, but if you harvest every blade, you'll cheat nature—and yourself—of a new crop. In addition, please be considerate of others' property and do not go foraging on private land without the owners' permission. And keep in mind that most state and national parks have strict rules

regarding harvesting of plant materials, so be sure to check before you find yourself facing stiff fines.

## Air Drying

The least-expensive and simplest way to dry many plants is to expose them to warm, dry, slowly circulating air. Because bright plant colors tend to fade when they're placed in direct sunlight, air drying should take place in an area that is also relatively dark: an attic, an uncluttered garage or outbuilding, or even an airy guest bedroom with closed curtains. Adequate ventilation is a must. Basements with poor air circulation just won't do because their damp, cool conditions foster molds and mildew.

*Dried flowers and herbs seem to arrange themselves when you place them in a pretty basket.*

*Your attic is the perfect place to air-dry herbs. These bunches have been fastened with rubber bands and hooked through hanging loops of string.*

## Hanging

The most convenient method of air drying plants is to suspend them upside down by their bundled stems. There are dozens of ways to do this, from hammering nails into exposed attic beams to constructing a series of crossbars in an empty room or shed. Many drying enthusiasts set up a special, horizontal support system by inserting two eye hooks, one into each of two opposite walls, and stringing a taut rope, wire, or chain between them. (Be sure the hooks pierce the wooden joists behind the walls, or your system may collapse, taking chunks of your walls along with it!) Chains work especially well because bunches of materials hooked into the individual links will stay in one place instead of sliding together as they tend to do on wires. You also may want to hang the bundles throughout your home; they'll shed a bit, but they're always attractive and often fragrant, too.

To assemble plant bunches for drying, strip the lowest leaves from the stems and cut the stems to even lengths. Using a tightly twisted rubber band, bind five to ten stems together, 1 or 2 inches from the cut ends. (Avoid combining different types of plants in a single bunch; they may dry at different rates.) Next, unbend a paper clip to form a hook. Slip one end of the hook through the rubber band and the other onto the rope, wire, or chain, leaving space between each bundle (see Figure 1 on the opposite page). Don't be tempted to substitute string or wire for the rubber bands. As the stems dry, they will shrink, and wire or string (unlike rubber bands) won't shrink with them.

Allow the plant materials to dry, checking on them every day or two until the petals or foliage feel papery and rigid or until the stems snap apart when bent. If you see signs of mildew or insect damage, remove and destroy the affected plants immediately. Depending on the types of materials you're drying, the size of the bundles, and the humidity in the environment, drying can take from four days to several weeks.

As a rule of thumb, air drying works best with materials that tend to hold their shapes when they dry naturally: grasses, seed heads, and cones, for example. Stems that bear spikes of flowers also take well to air drying when gathered in small clusters, but large blooms with many petals may fare less well.

Remove and store the bundles as soon as they're dry, or they'll become so fragile that you won't be able to work with them. Place the bunches in paper bags or cardboard boxes with lids and keep these containers in a cool, moisture-free location.

## Air Drying in Containers

Another air-drying technique, more suitable for long-stemmed weeds, grasses, and seedpods, consists of placing the materials upright in empty containers. Choose a sturdy vase or any container with an opening large enough to allow good air circulation around the stems and seed heads. Cut the stems to varying lengths so that the blooms won't touch one another (see Figure 2). Place the stems loosely in the container and set the container in a warm, dry, dark area.

Everlastings and blooms with very lightweight petals may also be dried by placing them in containers with a small amount of water. You'll enjoy their fresh-cut appearance as the water slowly evaporates, and after it has, the flowers may be left in the container to dry.

## Air Drying on Screens

A variation of air drying, this technique is best suited for flowers with especially fragile stems or with large heads that collapse inward when they're suspended upside down. Recycled window screens work well, but if you don't have any, don't despair. Making your own screens takes only an hour or two, a few scraps of lumber, a hammer, some nails, a staple gun, and some ¼-inch hardware cloth purchased from your local hardware store. Nail the lumber together to form a square or rectangular frame and then staple the screen to the frame (see Figure 3).

Position the screen parallel to the ground and at least one foot above the ground in any shaded, warm, dry location. To dry foliage, simply spread the leaves on the screen. When working with blooms, punch small holes in the screen, strip the leaves from the stems, and insert the stems all the

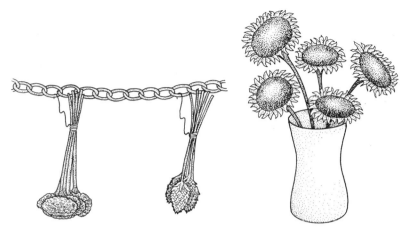

*Figure 1*                    *Figure 2*

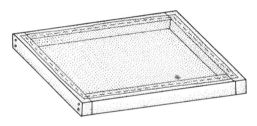

*Figure 3*

*Don't throw away that old clothes-drying rack— recycle it into the perfect support system for bundled, short-stemmed plants.*

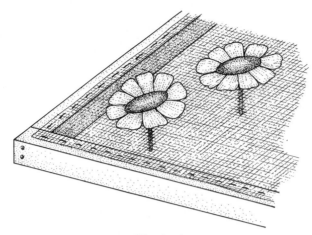

*Figure 4*

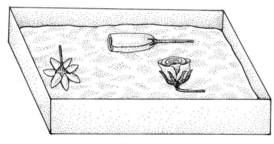

*Figure 5*

way through the holes until the back of each flower head is supported by the screen (see Figure 4). You also can cut off the stems and spread the blooms in a single layer on top of the screen, but turn the blooms over frequently to prevent the petals from curling excessively. Whichever screen-drying method you choose, be sure to leave plenty of space between the blooms; they shouldn't touch one another. Drying times will vary, but in many situations, 5 to 15 days will be adequate.

Screen-dried flowers without stems are perfect for hot-gluing into arrangements. In fact, even if you plan to dry bunches by suspending them from their stems, you may want to use the screen-drying method to accumulate an assortment of blooms just for this purpose.

Weak stems may also be reinforced before the flower is dried. Cut the stem off to ½ inch below the flower. Then insert a piece of medium-gauge floral wire up through the remaining stem and on through the center of the flower. Bend a

small hook into the upper end of the wire and pull the wire back into the flower until the hook is buried. Secure the wire to the short stem by wrapping them both with floral tape and poke the stem down through the screen. This technique works well with strawflowers and Queen-Anne's-lace.

The black, plastic plant trays found at greenhouses also work in a pinch; just insert the stems into their drainage holes and allow the plant materials to dry.

## Drying with Desiccants

Desiccants are substances that absorb moisture and are most often used to dry very delicate flowers such as calendula, roses, and zinnias. The most common desiccant, one used by professionals and hobbyists alike, is silica gel. It is available from florists, craft shops, and many garden-supply centers. Silica gel, which looks very much like white sand, contains small crystals of cobalt chloride; these crystals change color as they absorb moisture.

When working with silica gel, always wear a dust mask, and never, under any circumstances, use silica gel to dry materials that will be eaten. The gel is toxic and may absorb pesticides from roadside- or garden-plant materials!

To prepare blooms for drying, cut the stems as short as possible. Spread ½ to 1 inch of silica gel in the bottom of a shallow container and arrange the blooms on top; leave plenty of space between the blooms and limit yourself to a single type of bloom in each container. Flat-faced flowers, such as daisies, should be positioned face down; rounded flowers, face up. Spiked flowers and those with bell or trumpet shapes dry best when placed on their sides (see Figure 5).

Using great care, cover the flowers with another ½ inch of silica gel, making sure that the flower beneath isn't crumpled or wrinkled. (Depending on the depth of your container, you may create up to three layers of blooms and gel.) Place a tight-fitting lid on the container and set it aside.

Check the contents once every three days until the blooms feel dry to the touch. You'll know you've let the blooms dry too long if they crumble when they're handled.

When the flowers have dried, carefully pour off the silica gel until the flowers are revealed, then transfer the flowers to a flat work surface. To remove any residual dust, brush the dried blooms lightly with a soft artist's brush.

Silica gel may be reused many times. When it begins to change color (the manufacturer's instructions will describe these changes), pour it into a shallow pan and bake it at 225°F for 20 minutes to remove all the moisture. Allow the gel to cool and store it in an airtight container.

Desiccant-dried plant materials reabsorb moisture much more readily than you might wish, so display your finished projects only during the driest months of the year. During humid months, pack the projects in dark plastic bags or cardboard boxes, adding some silica gel to the bottom as added protection. Another way to keep desiccant-dried materials in good shape is to spray the dried materials with two or three coats of clear lacquer or with any clear, airtight sealant.

Another common desiccant mixture consists of two parts borax and one part dry white sand. Before using this homemade mixture, remove all moisture from it by heating it for two hours in a 200°F oven. Cool the mixture, store it in airtight containers, and use it just as you would use silica gel. Sand, cat box litter, and cornmeal will also work as desiccants, but because these materials are much heavier than silica gel, you run the risk of damaging delicate blooms.

## Drying in the Microwave

Used in conjunction with silica gel, a microwave oven can speed up the drying process considerably. Unfortunately, because these miraculous machines vary so widely in their wattage, settings, and performance, you'll need to experiment several times with

each material. Don't forget to record the results in your notebook so you'll know what to expect the next time around. Also remember that microwaving will remove the fragrance from most materials.

Prepare a nonmetal container by spreading a thin layer of silica gel on its bottom. Arrange the blooms as you would for ordinary, silica-gel drying. Then spread a thin layer of gel over and between the blooms. If your microwave has settings ranging from one to ten, set it at four (about 300 watts); if it has only three or four settings, set it at half power (about 350 watts); and if it has only high and defrost settings, use the defrost setting (about 200 watts).

As a rule of thumb, one or more blooms or pieces of foliage in ½ pound of silica gel will take about 2 to 2½ minutes to dry. If you find that you have overdried the materials, try another batch, decreasing the heating time by 20 seconds. If the materials aren't sufficiently dry, heat the next batch for an additional 15 seconds. Establishing the required heating times for

*Forget the popcorn; instead, pop in your plants. Your family microwave is a great nature-craft tool for drying plant materials.*

*When you want picture-perfect dried materials, choose an electric dehydrator. It's perfectly suited for drying fruit slices and many-petaled flowers, such as roses.*

upon the material, so start with 1 minute and then add more heating time in 20-second increments.

## Drying in the Oven

Oven drying is especially effective for rapid drying of fruit slices and large flowers with many petals. Set the oven at 175°F, place the flowers or fruit face up on the oven racks, and bake the materials, with the oven door cracked, for three to ten hours. Be sure to place a cookie sheet or shallow pan beneath the racks to catch any leaking juices. Remove the materials before they have dried completely and allow them to finish drying on a screen or a rack in a warm, dry, dark room.

## Drying in an Electric Dehydrator

For the serious nature crafter, an electric dehydrator can prove to be a real boon. These tidy, energy-efficient contraptions are manufactured in sizes that will fit on any kitchen countertop or table. Although models are constructed differently, their basic operating theory is the same. When the machine is turned on, it circulates evenly heated air, usually through a number of stacked trays.

Dehydrators are handy for air-drying slices of sugar-laden fruits that might otherwise attract insects and that have an irritating tendency to scorch in traditional ovens.

## Preserving with Glycerin

Glycerin preservation—a method by which the natural moisture in plant materials is replaced with a preservative—isn't exactly a drying method, but it serves the same purpose. Plant materials preserved in this fashion retain an almost-fresh appearance and texture.

For instructions on how to preserve green or autumn leaves with glycerin, see "Leaves" on page 165. Evergreen foliage and grasses may also be preserved with glycerin. Although evergreen foliage may be harvested at any time, it does best when it's harvested in late summer.

different materials will definitely require experimentation.

After heating, remove the container and allow it to stand undisturbed for about 10 minutes (for fragile blooms) or up to 30 minutes (for sturdier blooms). Place a lid on the container during this time, cracking it slightly to allow moisture to escape.

Microwave ovens also do an excellent job of drying materials without silica gel. Place the materials on a paper towel and cover them with another paper towel before heating. Especially juicy materials, such as citrus slices, may require two or three layers of paper towels underneath, and you may need to replace the dampened sheets with dry ones about halfway through the drying process. Another method of absorbing released moisture is to place the fresh materials inside a flat paper bag, fold the bag once to close it loosely, and then place it over a microwave-safe container so that the leaking juices will be contained. Drying times will vary greatly depending

Grasses can be harvested just as they begin to bloom and woody-stemmed foliage just as the leaves mature.

To prepare woody stems, make a solution of two parts hot water to one part glycerin and mix it thoroughly. Cut a ½-inch slit at the bottom of the stem and immediately place the stem in about 3 inches of this solution. Leave the container in a warm, dry place, out of direct sunlight. As the moisture in the plant evaporates, the solution will be drawn up the stem and into the leaves and blooms. Maintain the original liquid level by topping off with additional solution as necessary. Depending on the thickness of the leaves, the entire process will take between four days and four weeks. Remove the stems before oily drops of the solution begin to appear on the leaves. The glycerin solution may be strained and reused several times.

The same glycerin solution works well with seed heads and grasses, but it should be cooled before the stems are placed into it. These materials should be removed somewhat sooner—usually within two days. To dye plant materials, add food coloring to the solution.

Plants preserved with glycerin do tend to reabsorb moisture, so keep any arrangements in which they're used away from high-humidity environments. Do not, however, store them in airtight containers because moisture in the materials may condense and cause mildew and molds. Perforated cardboard boxes that are kept in a dry location are ideal.

# Plants for Drying

| MATERIAL | HARVEST HINTS | DRYING METHODS |
|---|---|---|
| Anise hyssop | Cut flower stalks when in full bloom. | Hang in bunches. |
| Apple | Purchase only unblemished, ripe fruit. Slice horizontally to show starlike pattern created by seeds; slice vertically to accentuate apple silhouette. | Dry in oven. Soak $\frac{1}{8}$- to $\frac{1}{4}$-inch-wide slices for 15 minutes in mixture of 1 tablespoon of fresh lemon juice, 1 tablespoon of commercial fruit preservative, and 1 quart of water. Pat dry and bake on waxed paper–lined cookie sheets at 200°F for 2 hours, turning frequently. Dry in microwave without silica gel. Complete drying on racks or screens. |
| Artemisia | Harvest anytime. | Dry upright in containers. Hang in small bunches. |
| Baby's-breath | Gather at full-bloom stage. | Dry upright in containers. Hang in small bunches. |
| Basil | Cut stems before plants bloom. | Hang in small bunches. Dry leaves on screens. Dry leaves in microwave without silica gel for about 1 minute. |
| Bay | Harvest anytime. | Dry leaves on screens. Hang in bunches. |
| Bee balm | Cut stems right after blooms open. | Hang in bunches. Dry in microwave without silica gel. |
| Black-eyed Susan | Gather at full-bloom stage. | Dry on screens. |
| Borage | Harvest leaves anytime; cut bloom stems just after peak-bloom stage. | Dry in silica gel for best color retention. Dry blooms face down on screens. |
| Boxwood | Pick from late summer through winter. | Allow to dry in place in the arrangement or wreath. Preserve with glycerin. |
| Calendula | Harvest after blooms open. | Dry single blooms face down on screens. Dry in silica gel. Dry in microwave with or without silica gel. Dry in electric dehydrator. |

| MATERIAL | HARVEST HINTS | DRYING METHODS |
|---|---|---|
| **Carnation** | Cut blooms as soon as they open. | Dry blooms and leaves on screens.<br>Dry in microwave with silica gel.<br>Dry in electric dehydrator. |
| **Catnip** | Harvest leaves when young; blooms just after they've opened. | Hang in bunches.<br>Dry leaves in microwave without silica gel for 1½ minutes.<br>Dry leaves on screens. (Lock up your cats!) |
| **Chili pepper** | Pick or purchase unblemished, ripe peppers. | Dry in oven. Cut small slit in each pepper and bake at 175°F on cookie sheet lined with waxed paper for 10 hours. Turn periodically.<br>Dry in microwave without silica gel. Pierce in several places with needle before starting. Cook between single layers of paper towels.<br>Dry in electric dehydrator.<br>Hang in bunches. |
| **Chinese lantern** | Gather stems when calyxes (bases) are open or closed. | Dry upright in containers.<br>Dry on screens after reinforcing stems with floral wire. |
| **Chrysanthemum** | Harvest before flower centers have completely opened. | Dry on screens.<br>Dry in silica gel.<br>Dry in electric dehydrator. |
| **Citrus fruit** | Purchase only unblemished, ripe fruit. | Dry in oven. Cut into ⅛- to ¼-inch-thick slices. Bake on unlined cookie sheets at 200°F until completely dry. Do not allow to brown; turn frequently.<br>Dry in microwave. Arrange slices on 3 layers of paper towels, covering with 2 more layers. Complete drying process on screens or racks. |
| **Cockscomb** | Cut at full-bloom stage. | Hang in small bunches after stripping away foliage.<br>Dry blooms on screens. |
| **Coneflower** | Harvest seed heads when petals have fallen, and flowers are at peak-bloom stage. | Hang in bunches.<br>Dry upright in containers.<br>Dry in microwave set at low. |

*(continued on next page)*

# Plants for Drying—Continued

| MATERIAL | HARVEST HINTS | DRYING METHODS |
|---|---|---|
| Cotton lavender | Gather at full-bloom stage. | Hang in bunches. |
| Daisy | Gather anytime between bud and bloom stages. | Dry on screens. Dry face down in silica gel. Dry in microwave without silica gel. |
| Feverfew | Harvest at peak-bloom stage. | Hang in bunches. Dry separated blooms and leaves on screens. Dry blooms or leaves in silica gel. Dry in microwave without silica gel for 1½ minutes. |
| Geranium, scented | Harvest when mature. | Dry on screens. Dry in microwave. |
| Globe amaranth | Collect main flower heads as they open; replace stems with wires unless you plan to dry heads in microwave. (Never place wire-fortified stems in microwave.) | Hang in bunches. Dry on screens. Dry in microwave without silica gel. |
| Globe thistle | Pick at full-bloom stage. | Hang in bunches. Dry upright in containers. Dry mature leaves in silica gel. |
| Goldenrod | Gather when florets are still closed. | Hang in bunches. Dry upright in containers. Dry in microwave without silica gel. |
| Gourd and pumpkin | Cut from vines when stems turn brown and gourd is fully mature, leaving short length of stem attached; do not use wax-coated gourds because they will rot when air-dried—grow them yourself or purchase them at local market. | Air-dry. Rinse in solution of warm water and mild detergent. Then rinse in clean water. Place in solution of 1 part bleach to 2 parts water for 20 minutes to kill bacteria that might cause fruit to rot. Remove from bleach solution and allow to dry in any warm, dry location. Dry in microwave for 15 minutes at low setting after drilling ½-inch hole in each end. |
| Grass | Harvest at flowering stage. | Hang in bunches. Dry upright in containers. |

| MATERIAL | HARVEST HINTS | DRYING METHODS |
|---|---|---|
| Hydrangea | Harvest blooms in autumn, just after buds in centers have fallen free of flowers. | Dry upright in containers.<br>Dry in microwave without silica gel. |
| Larkspur | Cut just as blooms begin to open. | Hang in bunches.<br>Dry upright in containers.<br>Dry in microwave without silica gel. |
| Lavender | Harvest at full-bloom stage. | Hang in bunches.<br>Dry on screens.<br>Do not microwave. |
| Lemon balm | Harvest leaves for culinary use before bloom stage; blooms do not dry well; flower stalks will retain shapes if cut when blooms first open. | Hang in bunches.<br>Dry detached leaves on screens.<br>Dry leaves in microwave without silica gel. |
| Lemon verbena | Harvest leaves anytime; cut bloom stems when blooms start to open. | Hang in small bunches. |
| Love-in-a-mist | Cut stems as soon as they mature. | Hang in bunches.<br>Dry upright in containers. |
| Magnolia | Collect branches of mature leaves anytime. | Preserve with glycerin. |
| Marigold | Gather at full-bloom stage. | Dry on screens.<br>Dry in silica gel.<br>Dry in electric dehydrator.<br>Dry in microwave without silica gel. |
| Marjoram | Cut at peak-bloom stage. | Dry leaves on screens.<br>Hang in bunches.<br>Dry in microwave without silica gel. |
| Mint | Harvest leaves for culinary use before bloom stage; harvest blooms at peak-bloom stage. | Hang in bunches.<br>Dry detached leaves on screens.<br>Dry stems upright in containers.<br>Dry in microwave without silica gel. |

(continued on next page)

# Plants for Drying—Continued

| MATERIAL | HARVEST HINTS | DRYING METHODS |
|---|---|---|
| Money plant | Cut midsummer to late summer. | Hang in bunches. When plants are dry, peel off outer coating of each seed pod until only papery, white lining remains. |
| Mushroom | Pick or purchase unblemished specimens. | Dry in oven. Spread on cookie rack with pan underneath to catch juices. Bake at 200°F for 2 to 3 hours. |
| Okra | Purchase only unblemished specimens. | After piercing both ends with fork, heat for 3 minutes in microwave. Complete drying on screens or racks.<br><br>Dry in electric dehydrator. |
| Pearly everlasting | Gather before flowers have opened completely. | Hang in bunches. |
| Pomegranate | Purchase only unblemished, ripe fruit. | Dry whole fruit on screens. Use skewer to poke several holes in blossom end, then use needle to punch many holes through skin. Place tray underneath to catch leaking juices. Dry for up to 1 month. Fruit may also be sliced in half, cleaned out, screen-dried, and hot-glued back together. |
| Poppy | Harvest blooms at full-bloom stage and seed heads when hard and mature. | Hang in bunches.<br>Preserve with glycerin.<br>Dry seed heads by placing stems upright in containers.<br>Dry in microwave without silica gel. |
| Purple coneflower | Cut at peak-bloom stage. | Dry in silica gel for best color retention.<br>Dry on screens.<br>Hang individual stems. |
| Queen-Anne's-lace | Harvest leaves anytime; cut bloom stems before plant goes to seed. | Hang in bunches.<br>Dry on screens, or upright in containers.<br>Dry in silica gel. |

| MATERIAL | HARVEST HINTS | DRYING METHODS |
|---|---|---|
| Raspberry | Gather just before fully ripened. | Dry on screens with stems attached. <br> Dry in electric dehydrator. |
| Rose | Harvest buds when they are tight or just slightly open, blooms just before full-bloom stage, and petals at full-bloom stage. | Dry buds or petals on screens. <br> Dry blooms in silica gel for best color retention. <br> Dry blooms in oven. <br> Dry blooms and buds in electric dehydrator. <br> Dry blooms and buds in microwave set at low. |
| Rosemary | Harvest when mature. | Hang in bunches. <br> Dry stems on screens. |
| Sage | Cut foliage anytime; cut blooms at peak. | Hang in bunches. <br> Dry upright in containers. <br> Dry leaves in microwave without silica gel. |
| Seeds: melon and squash | Scoop from ripe fruit. | Dry in microwave. First soak in solution of $\frac{1}{2}$ cup of bleach and 1 quart of water for 20 minutes. Rinse, pat dry, and arrange in single layers between paper towels. Heat at half power for 5 minutes, turning once halfway through. <br> Dry on screens and then in oven. Rinse first, screen-dry, and bake at 200°F for 25 minutes. |
| Squash | Purchase only unblemished fruit. | Dry slices in microwave between 2 paper towels. |
| Statice | Gather at full-bloom stage. | Hang in bunches. <br> Dry in microwave without silica gel. |
| Strawflower | Collect main flower heads as they begin to open. | Dry on screens, either removing stems entirely or fortifying them with floral wire. <br> Dry in microwave, placing bloom face down, without silica gel. (Never place wire-fortified stems in microwave.) |

(continued on next page)

# Plants for Drying—Continued

| MATERIAL | HARVEST HINTS | DRYING METHODS |
|---|---|---|
| Sunflower | Cut before fully mature. | Hang in bunches of 3 to 5 flower heads.<br>Dry on screens.<br>Dry in oven, removing stems first and baking on oven rack at 150°F for about 8 hours. |
| Sweet Annie | Harvest before or after seed stage. | Hang in bunches.<br>Dry on screens. |
| Thyme | Harvest blooms at peak-bloom stage. Harvest leaves for culinary use before bloom stage. | Hang in bunches.<br>Dry on screens.<br>Dry in microwave without silica gel. |
| Yarrow | Harvest at peak-bloom stage. | Hang in small bunches.<br>Dry on screens after removing leaves from stems.<br>Dry in microwave without silica gel. |
| Zinnia | Gather at full-bloom stage. | Dry on screens.<br>Dry in silica gel.<br>Dry in electric dehydrator. |

*You don't need a barn full of dried materials to make these quick-and-easy corsages. Each corsage needs just a handful of stems for eye-catching results.*

# Miniature Dried Flower Corsages

## WHAT YOU NEED (for each corsage)

Assorted dried materials as listed under the individual corsages that follow

Small, dried ivy leaves

3 inches of medium-gauge floral wire

Green floral tape

Hot-glue gun and glue sticks

4-inch-diameter cotton or paper doily

Corsage pin (available from florists and craft-supply stores)

## INDIVIDUAL CORSAGE MATERIALS

### Cockscomb Corsage

1 stem of dried pink statice,
2½ inches long

3 stems of dried oregano, 2 inches long

1 stem of dried burgundy cockscomb,
2 inches long

### Ivy Corsage

2 stems of dried miniature ivy,
4½ inches long

2 stems of dried ivy, 3 inches long

1 stem of dried yarrow, dyed red,
2 inches long

3 assorted cones and pods on wires
(see Step 4 of the "S-Curve Cone
Centerpiece" on page 55)

1 yard of red satin ribbon, ¼ inch wide,
tied into a bow

### Gardenia Corsage

1 stem of dried mint blooms,
1½ inches long

3 stems of dried lavender,
2 to 3 inches long

4 silk gardenias, 1 to 2½ inches long

2 artificial bluebird feathers (available
at craft-supply stores)

### Black-Eyed Susan Corsage

5 dried red chili peppers, 2 inches long

1 dried black-eyed Susan, 2¾ inches long

5 stems of dried oregano, 2½ inches long

2 dried ivy leaves

1 dried black-eyed Susan flower head

1 piece of red netting, 2 inches square

### Larkspur Corsage

2 stems of dried purple statice,
2½ inches long

3 stems of dried red globe amaranths,
1½ to 2 inches long

1 stem of larkspur, dried in silica gel

2 sprigs of dried baby's-breath,
1½ to 2½ inches long

## WHAT YOU DO

1 Gather the dried materials into a small cluster. Straighten the floral wire and place it parallel to the stems of the dried materials so that about ½ inch of wire overlaps ½ inch of the stem ends. Wrap the wire and stems together with green floral tape, spiraling the tape downward to cover the entire length of the wire. Then, starting from the bottom, shape the free end of the wire to resemble a curled stem.

2 Hot-glue the back of the taped cluster to the center of the cotton or paper doily. Then hot-glue one or more ivy leaves to the base of the flower cluster on the front of the doily. Hot-glue the additional decorations listed for the individual corsages in place; then hot-glue the corsage pin to the back of the doily.

# "Forever Yours" Wedding Bouquet

## WHAT YOU NEED

18 stems of glycerin-preserved eucalyptus:
one 12 inches long, one 8 inches long,
eight 6 inches long, and eight 4 inches long

1 handful of wild grass

6 stems of peppergrass, 3½ inches long

5 stems of purple statice, 3½ inches long

7 stems of white statice, 3½ inches long

50 strawflowers, in various colors and sizes

Plastic bouquet holder with dry floral foam

9-inch-diameter lace collar

White floral tape

About 50 floral picks

Hot-glue gun and glue sticks

12 strands of white faux 4 mm pearls, two 18
inches long and ten 8 inches long (available
at craft-supply and fabric stores)

2 yards of white lace ribbon, 1 inch wide

2 yards of cranberry ribbon, ½ inch wide

2 yards of purple ribbon, ¼ inch wide

About 3 inches of white, medium-gauge
floral wire

## WHAT YOU DO

*1* Insert the bouquet holder into the lace
collar and use white floral tape to secure
the collar tails to the handle of the holder.

*2* As you follow this step, think of the front
of the bouquet as the face of a clock.
Insert four of the 6-inch-long eucalyptus
stems into the foam at the three, six, nine,
and twelve o'clock positions. Insert the
remaining four 6-inch-long stems between
these. Then insert the 4-inch-long eucalyptus
stems throughout the bouquet.

*3* Insert half of the wild grass, spreading it
throughout the bouquet. Also insert the
peppergrass stems around the outer circumfer-

*A Victorian bride might
very well have picked and
dried the strawflowers for
her wedding bouquet.*

ence of the bouquet and the stems of purple and white statice throughout the bouquet.

**4** Set aside five or six strawflowers for use in Step 5. Attach a floral pick to the stem of each remaining bloom and add these strawflowers to the bouquet, placing the largest ones in the center of the bouquet and the smallest at the outer edges.

**5** To make a cascade, hot-glue the set-aside strawflowers onto the 12-inch-long eucalyptus stem, positioning the smallest strawflower bloom at the tail end of the eucalyptus. Then insert both the 8-inch-long and the 12-inch-long eucalyptus stems at the bottom of the bouquet, placing the long stem behind the short one.

**6** Place two 8-inch lengths of pearls together side-by-side, attach a floral

pick, and wrap the pick with white floral tape. Do the same with the two 18-inch lengths of pearls. Insert the picks into the bottom of the bouquet at the center.

**7** Using the three lengths of ribbon, make a simple two-loop bow, securing its center with a short piece of white floral wire (see "Two-Loop Bow" on page 52). Attach a floral pick to the wired center of the bow and wrap the pick with white floral tape. Then insert the picked bow behind the long eucalyptus stems so that the strings of pearls are in the center of the bow.

**8** Attach a floral pick to each of the eight remaining 8-inch lengths of pearls, wrap the picks with floral tape, and insert these throughout the bouquet. Then insert the remaining wild grass.

# Victorian Wreath

## WHAT YOU NEED

36 stems of sweet Annie, each about 12 inches long

12-inch-diameter grapevine wreath base, made with narrow vines

2 stems of mountain daisies, 24 to 36 blooms per stem

2 hydrangea flower heads, broken into small pieces

20 pink globe amaranths

20 purple globe amaranths

2 straight, $\frac{1}{4}$-inch-diameter twigs, $2\frac{1}{2}$ inches long

10 glycerin-preserved fern fronds, 8 inches long*

Pruning shears

Floral picks

Green floral tape

Wide-tipped felt marker

Hot-glue gun and glue sticks

$2\frac{1}{3}$ yards of light green organdy ribbon, $1\frac{1}{2}$ inches wide

$2\frac{1}{3}$ yards of dark green organdy ribbon, $1\frac{1}{2}$ inches wide

*You can purchase glycerin-preserved materials from craft-supply stores and mail-order suppliers, or you can preserve the materials yourself (see "Preserving with Glycerin" on page 78 and "Preserving Leaves" on page 165).

## WHAT YOU DO

**1** Using the pruning shears, cut 6 to 8 stems of sweet Annie, each about 4 to 6 inches long, and gather them into a cluster. Attach a floral pick to the cluster and secure it by wrapping the pick and the stems with green floral tape. Repeat this step to make as many clusters as the 36 stems will provide.

**2** Using the wide-tipped felt marker, mark the front top and front bottom

of the grapevine wreath base to create reference points for your design.

**3** Starting at the bottom of the wreath base and continuing up one side and then the other, hot-glue the picked sweet Annie to the base. The picked ends of each cluster should be at the top so that the bloom ends of succeeding clusters will hide the picks of those already attached. (In Step 6 you'll cover the space where the picked stems meet at the top of the wreath.)

**4** Remove the mountain daisies from their stems. Then hot-glue these flower heads, the hydrangea pieces, and the pink and purple amaranths to the sweet Annie, taking care to fill in all the spaces on the wreath base.

**5** On each side of the wreath, just below the center, slide in one of the straight twigs. Check to be sure the twigs are even with each other. Then remove them, apply hot-glue to each, and reinsert them into the wreath.

**6** Cut a 1⅓ yard length of the light green ribbon and a 1⅓-yard length of the dark green ribbon. Place the two pieces back to back and form a single bow with the doubled ribbons (see "Two-Loop Bow" on page 52). Hot-glue the bow to the top center of the wreath, over the picked stems of sweet Annie.

**7** Cut the remaining ribbon into four equal lengths and make a deep V-shaped cut at every end. Pair one light green ribbon to each dark green ribbon and place them back to back.

**8** Using one of the pairs of ribbons, first hot-glue a V-shaped end onto the outer, protruding end of a twig, allowing the ribbon to extend 3 inches beyond the end of the twig. Then, working toward the wreath, hot-glue the ribbon in loops to the twig, covering each glue spot with the succeeding loop. When you reach the wreath, loop and hot-glue the ribbon one more time, and then bring it up to the bow and hot-glue it in place. Repeat with the other ribbon pair and the other twig.

*A dramatic organdy ribbon and a delicate blend of colorful dried blooms highlight this beautiful wreath.*

# Rose-Bead Necklace

*Traditional rose-bead recipes call for salt, but the designer who created these beads tells us that salt attracts moisture and prevents rose beads from drying.*

## WHAT YOU NEED (for 2 necklaces)

2 gallons of fresh rose petals

Pruning shears

Old-fashioned, manual meat grinder with fine meat-cutting blade

Refrigerator container with lid

72 T-pins

1 large sheet of cork board or thick cardboard

Shallow cardboard tray or airy containers, like berry boxes

Sewing needle with large eye

Nylon bead-stringing thread (FF gauge) or carpet and button thread

Scissors

2 bead tips

Hot-glue gun and glue sticks

Needle-nose pliers

29 gold rondelle beads

2 jump rings

2-piece barrel clasp

## WHAT YOU DO

**1** Unless you have an acre's worth of roses, you'll need to collect these blooms a few at a time. Start on a clear, sunny day, after the morning dew has evaporated. Using the pruning shears, harvest well-opened blooms rather than the buds.

**2** After collecting the flowers, gently remove the petals and, using the meat grinder and the finest meat-cutting blade that you have, grind the petals thoroughly into a paste. Store the ground petals in a sealed container in the refrigerator, adding petals each day as you collect and grind them.

**3** After you've collected and ground at least 2 gallons of petals, regrind the paste 15 to 20 times. Yes, patience is required. Your goal is to produce a paste that

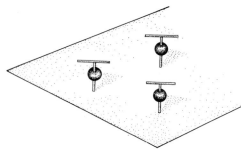

*Figure 1*

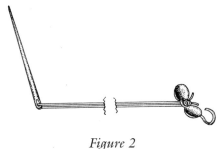

*Figure 2*

is as fine and malleable as clay. Test the paste occasionally by trying to roll a small amount of it into a ball. When the paste will hold its shape, you can start to shape the beads.

4 Shape the rose-petal paste into beads by rolling marble-size lumps of it into balls. (Keep in mind that your beads will shrink considerably as they cure: A marble-size moist bead will turn into a pea-size dry bead.) Place the lump of paste in the palm of one hand and roll it around with the fingertips of your other hand as if you were rolling a small meatball. One warning: Rose paste stains, so wear your oldest clothes and don't work over a linen tablecloth!

5 To create holes in the beads, gently insert a T-pin through the center of each bead while the bead is still moist. Position the pierced bead in the center of the pin shaft and insert the pin into a sheet of corkboard or cardboard (see Figure 1). Make sure that the bottom of the bead doesn't touch the surface of the board or the bead will dry flat at that end.

6 Place the bead-covered board in a dry, warm area. (Believe it or not, your family car provides an excellent drying environment when parked in the summer sun. In fact, the upholstery will retain the wonderful fragrance of roses for weeks.) Using your fingertips, rotate the beads occasionally so that they don't stick to the T-pins as they dry. Unless the humidity is high, the beads will dry in about one week.

7 When the beads are dry, remove them from the pins and spread them out in an uncovered cardboard tray or in airy containers. Allow the inner surfaces of the pinholes to dry for another day or two.

8 Thread the needle with the nylon bead-stringing thread and double the thread, cutting the ends of the thread so that the length of doubled thread is several inches longer than the desired length of your necklace.

9 Insert the needle through the hole in one bead tip. Tie a knot at the end of the thread and, using the scissors, trim the thread ends from the knot (see Figure 2). Pull the knot tightly against the inner surface of the bead tip. Apply a little hot glue to the knot itself and use a pair of pliers to close the end of the bead tip around the knot.

10 Starting with a gold rondelle bead, alternately string the rondelles and rose beads onto the thread until the necklace is the desired length. If you wish, vary the sizes of the necklace beads, stringing the larger ones in the center of the necklace.

11 Repeat Step 9 to add the other bead tip to the opposite end of the necklace. Then slip a jump ring through each bead tip and close the rings with the pliers. Finally, slip the barrel clasp sections onto the jump rings and close the clasp sections with the pliers.

*For additional information on using rose petals, see "Pressed Flowers & Herbs" on page 190.*

# E EVERGREENS

When most people hear the word "evergreens," the first thing they think of is a "wreath." Certainly, a holiday wreath made with fragrant pine boughs and red holly berries is a Christmas staple. But evergreens can make just as enduring an impression in summer, spring, or fall when they are combined in appealing ways with dried flowers, fruits, and other seasonal natural materials.

Evergreens grow in abundance and in a wide range of shapes and colors—at least a dozen shades of green, in fact. But what evergreens have in common is the truth behind their name: They are available for use all year long. Stroll through the woods or around your yard, and you will see for yourself how diverse this group of perennials really is. Take along your pruning shears and cut a variety of evergreens to use at home.

Many types of evergreens are also available for purchase in craft-supply stores and discount outlets. Sometimes these materials are sprayed with paint to heighten their color, or they are preserved with glycerin to help them remain supple and retain much of their natural color and shape. To learn how to preserve your materials with glycerin at home, see "Preserving Leaves" on page 165 and "Preserving with Glycerin" on page 78.

If you work with fresh-cut evergreens, you can let some of them dry in place. Bay leaves, boxwood, cedar, eucalyptus, fir, and ivy do especially well. But just like your favorite Christmas tree, most evergreens will become overly dry and brittle in a few weeks. Ask your local nursery to suggest which evergreens in your part of the country will hold up the longest after they are cut.

You can make a wreath or swag by using evergreens as the main materials covering the base and other materials as accents. Or you can reverse this ratio so that the evergreens are the accent to a predominately floral arrangement. Wreaths made from evergreens can be assembled in three ways: (1) If you are working with strong-stemmed evergreens, such as firs, cut the stems at an angle and insert them directly into a straw, polystyrene, or grapevine base. If you use a grapevine base, you will need to hot-glue the stems between the vine strands (see "Christmas Wreath" on the opposite page). (2) If the stems are more delicate, trim them short, attach them in small groups to floral picks, and insert them into the base. (3) You can also wire clusters of stems to a wire ring base or hot-glue individual leaves to a grapevine, polystyrene, or straw base.

## How to Keep Evergreens Supple

Here are two ways to keep your cut evergreens supple longer:

- Before attaching the evergreens, dip them in a bucket containing a mixture of four parts water to one part acrylic floor wax. Shake off the excess and let the needles dry before using the branches. Use the same mixture in a spray mister to apply to the finished arrangement. This technique works well on ferns and leaves, too.

- Mist your finished arrangement weekly with water from a quart spray bottle into which you've mixed half a teaspoon of liquid fabric softener.

# Christmas Wreath

## WHAT YOU NEED

12-inch-diameter straw wreath base

95 stems of blue spruce, 8 inches long

40 stems of hemlock with small cones still attached, 6 inches long

6 clusters of red bayberries, 2 inches long

8 stems of mountain holly, 3 inches long

7 sprigs of mistletoe with berries, 3 inches long

4 clusters of thistle berries, 2 inches long

3 white-pine cones

3 rose hips

3 large handfuls of Spanish moss

1 green chenille stem, 12 inches long

146 floral picks

Hot-glue gun and glue sticks

Floral pins

## WHAT YOU DO

*1* Fashion a hanger for your wreath with the chenille stem (see "Hangers" on page 118). Attach floral picks to all of the blue-spruce stems. Starting at the top of the wreath, insert each picked stem into the straw base at an angle, moving in a clockwise direction. Cover the entire base, including the inner and outer rims.

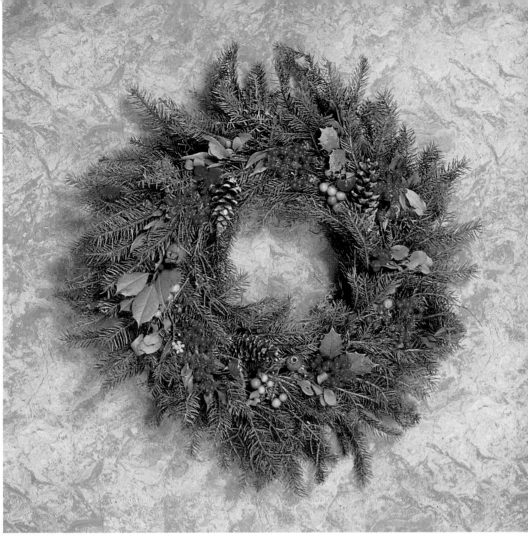

*Thistle berries and rose hips put a slightly different spin on a traditional holiday wreath of red and green.*

*2* Attach floral picks to the hemlock stems and insert them into the base at the same angle as the spruce stems. Make sure the small cones show. Fully cover the front of the wreath and the inner rim with the hemlock stems.

*3* Hot-glue the clusters of bayberries to the front of the wreath, spacing them about 3 inches apart; angle them as you did the evergreens. Attach picks to the holly stems and insert them around the front of the wreath in the same direction as the other materials.

*4* Hot-glue the mistletoe sprigs and the thistle berries, placing them between the bayberries. Hot-glue the white-pine cones 6 inches apart around the front of the wreath. Attach picks to the rose hips and insert them into the front of the wreath about 8 inches apart.

*5* Finish the wreath by covering the back with Spanish moss; use floral pins to hold the moss in place.

## Designer Tips

AS YOU WORK ON AN ARRANGEMENT, position the vase or container at a comfortable height. Using a high countertop or table will help you avoid back strain. For round arrangements, a lazy Susan will also come in handy; by placing the vase or container on it, you'll find it an easy matter to view your arrangement from every perspective. To check your arrangement as it takes shape, place it in its actual display location for a minute or two. Stand back to gauge the effect you're creating, return the arrangement to your work surface, and make adjustments as necessary.

WHEN YOU'RE WORKING WITH DRIED MATERIALS, you may want to fill your container with cut pieces of dry floral foam so that the inserted stems will be held securely in position. To disguise any portions of foam that are likely to be visible when the arrangement has been completed, cover the foam with moss. Or if your dried materials are heavier than your container, fill the bottom third of the container with sand or rocks before starting.

ARRANGEMENTS ARE USUALLY STARTED by creating an outline with the tallest materials. Other materials, which provide color and texture, are then added one at a time to fill in the design.

MANY FLORAL DESIGNERS ADD MATERIALS IN "TRIANGLES." That is, they position dried or fresh flowers in sets of three so that the completed arrangement consists of a series of visual triangles, each of which is placed in a different position and some of which overlap.

KEEP IN MIND THAT darker colors, large blooms, and dense foliage will appear heavier than pale colors, small blooms, and fine-textured foliage. Round shapes hold attention, and spiky shapes lead the eye away. Your goal is to create an arrangement that first catches the viewer's attention at one focal point and then leads that attention throughout the display. In general, you should place larger, darker materials toward the center and base of your arrangement and smaller, lighter materials at the edges.

WHEN WORKING WITH FRESH FLOWERS, pick them either early or late in the day. Strip the lowest leaves from the stems and use a sharp knife to cut the stems at an angle. Then place the stems in warm water and allow them to stand for an hour or two. When you're ready to start your arrangement, fill your display container with a solution of flower preservative and water and recut the stems before placing them in the solution. You should avoid submerging the leaves and crowding the stems, or your finished arrangement may develop mold.

TO REVIVE WILTING BLOOMS, remove the stems from the arrangement and recut them at an angle while holding them under water; this will release any air in them—air which might otherwise block the intake of water. Then place the recut stems in warm water and leave them for a few hours before rearranging them.

# Basket Arrangement

## WHAT YOU NEED

2 large handfuls of sphagnum moss

9 stems of dried 'Silver King' artemisia,
   17 to 20 inches long

15 stems of dried mountain mint,
   14 to 17 inches long

8 sprigs of baby's-breath,
   12 to 16 inches long

8 stems of dried goldenrod,
   11 to 14 inches long

9 stems of dried purple statice,
   11 to 14 inches long

8 stems of dried red cockscomb,
   9 to 12 inches long

7 stems of dried roses,
   14 to 17 inches long

Basket, 6½ inches deep
   and 8 inches in diameter

Several sheets of newspaper

Serrated knife

1 block of dry floral foam

Spray bottle filled with water

Pruning shears

Green floral tape

Heavy-gauge floral wire

Wire cutters

*Warm colors, like those in this rounded arrangement, are emphasized when set off against paler greens and grays.*

## WHAT YOU DO

*1* If your basket is loosely woven, line the bottom with newspaper to confine any shedding materials. Then use the serrated knife to cut sections of dry floral foam to fit inside the basket.

*2* Insert the foam pieces into the basket until they fit snugly enough to hold each other firmly inside. Note that the foam should not protrude above the top of the basket.

*3* Completely cover the foam with sphagnum moss, using the knife to tuck it in securely around the edges of the basket.

*4* To form the design outline for your arrangement and to provide its predominant background color, start with the feathery stems of 'Silver King' artemisia. First strip all leaves from the lower portion of each stem. Then mist the stems lightly with water to prevent the remaining leaves from crumbling as you handle them. Select several relatively tall stems, cut each stem end at an angle, and insert the cut stems into the foam at the center of the basket. Then cut and insert the remaining stems, working out toward the basket edge from front to back and from side to side, shortening the stem lengths as you move toward the edges. This will create a rounded effect in the completed arrangement. Be sure to aim every stem end toward an invisible center point in the middle of the basket so that the stems angle out toward the edges of the basket.

*5* To give the arrangement both body and fragrance, insert the stems of mountain mint next. Again, place the tallest stems toward the center of the basket and the shorter ones out toward the edges, aiming them at the invisible center point as you insert them.

*6* Complete the arrangement by inserting, in this order, the baby's-breath (for a light, feminine touch), the goldenrod (its yellow color will draw the eye), the purple statice (for its color), and the red cockscomb. You will need to fortify the weak stems of the cockscomb by using green floral tape to secure a length of heavy-gauge floral wire to each stem. Use the same technique to strengthen any weak stems of other materials as well.

## WHAT YOU DO

*1* Place the two lengths of ribbon back to back, and use the doubled lengths to tie a single bow around the narrow neck of the vase. Cut the ribbon ends to the desired lengths.

*2* Arrange all the dried materials to make a single bouquet, placing the tallest pieces toward the center and back and adding the shorter pieces around and in front of them. Insert the bouquet into the vase.

## Sugar Bowl Arrangement

## WHAT YOU NEED

1 handful of sheet moss

5 stems of dried pink larkspur,
    1½ to 5 inches long

12 sprigs of dried caspia, 4 inches long

10 stems of dried lavender,
    1½ to 3 inches long

1 dried blue hydrangea flower head

3 stems of dried red roses,
    1½ to 2½ inches long

3 dried rose leaves

Serrated knife

Dry floral foam

Sugar bowl

Hot-glue gun and glue sticks

Floral picks

Scissors

## WHAT YOU DO

*1* Using the serrated knife, cut the dry floral foam to fit snugly inside the sugar bowl. Insert the foam into the bowl and disguise its upper surface by hot-gluing the sheet moss to it. Use the knife to tuck the edges of the moss between the foam and bowl.

*2* Attach floral picks to two of the longest stems of pink larkspur. Insert these into the foam in the center of the sugar bowl.

*3* Combining the caspia and the lavender, make four small clusters, each a different length. Attach a floral pick to each cluster. Then insert the clusters into the foam, varying their angles.

*4* Gently divide the hydrangea flower head into small pieces and hot-glue these to the caspia, varying the placement heights and angles, as shown in the photograph on page 109.

*5* Insert the longest rose stem next to the larkspur and hot-glue it in place. Then insert and hot-glue another rose stem next to it.

*6* Hot-glue the remaining pink larkspur into the arrangement, placing a few stems in front of the two roses.

*7* Hot-glue the last rose in place, near the other roses, toward the front of the arrangement. Finally, hot-glue the rose leaves next to the two roses in the front of the arrangement.

## China Vase Arrangement

## WHAT YOU NEED

1 handful of sheet moss

15 sprigs of baby's-breath,
    2 to 4½ inches long

2 stems of dried blue delphinium,
    3 inches long

Serrated knife

Dry floral foam

China vase, 4 inches tall

Hot-glue gun and glue sticks

Scissors

Floral picks

**Pottery**

WHAT

1 handf

25 stem
4 to

25 stem
4 to

46 stem
3 to

9 sprigs
2 to

7 dried

Serrated

Dry flo

Pottery

Hot-glu

Scissors

Floral p

WHAT

1 Usin
flora
Then sha
candlestic
the sheet
edges of

2 Usin
17 s
stems of
mixed m
each clus

3 Inser
cover
center an

## WHAT YOU DO

**1** Using the serrated knife, cut a piece of dry floral foam to fit inside the vase with ½ inch of foam protruding from the top of the vase. Insert the foam into the vase and then hot-glue the sheet moss to the foam's upper surface. Tuck the edges of the moss between the vase and the foam or trim the edges off completely.

**2** Group the sprigs of baby's-breath into five small clusters and attach a floral pick to each one. Insert the tallest cluster in the center of the moss-covered foam and the remaining clusters throughout.

**3** Cut the delphinium buds off the stems and hot-glue them throughout the arrangement.

## Pottery Mug Arrangement

### WHAT YOU NEED

1 handful of sheet moss

15 stems of dried brome or other grass, 3 to 7 inches long

19 sprigs of dried white winged everlasting, 2 to 4 inches long

21 stems of dried statice, 2 to 4 inches long

7 dried ivy leaves

Serrated knife

Dry floral foam

Mug, 3½ inches tall

Hot-glue gun and glue sticks

Scissors

Floral picks

*Pottery mugs, creamers, and even candlesticks make convenient and attractive containers for miniature floral arrangements.*

# Copper Tea Kettle Arrangement

*Don't be timid about using nontraditional containers for your floral arrangements—your kitchen is probably filled with potential "vases" like this copper kettle.*

## WHAT YOU NEED

85 sprigs of dried sweet Annie, 4 inches long

13 stems of dried purple statice, $1\frac{1}{2}$ to 5 inches long

10 dried zinnia blooms, 1 to $2\frac{1}{2}$ inches in diameter

6 stems of dried button dahlias, $1\frac{1}{2}$ to 2 inches long

Copper tea kettle

Several sheets of newspaper

Serrated knife

Dry floral foam

Floral picks

Hot-glue gun and glue sticks

## WHAT YOU DO

*1* Fill the kettle with crumpled newspaper. Using the serrated knife, cut the dry floral foam to fit tightly into the opening of the kettle, shaping it to extend $1\frac{1}{2}$ inches above the opening.

*2* Divide the sweet Annie into 17 clusters, each containing five sprigs. Attach a floral pick to each cluster.

*3* Insert the picked clusters into the foam, starting in the center and gradually creating an arrangement that slopes downward and outward. Be careful not to hide the handle of the kettle.

*4* Hot-glue the purple statice throughout the arrangement, inserting a few of the stems in pairs. Then, using the photograph as a guide, hot-glue the zinnias in place, arranging them at different angles and varying the placement of different sizes. Finally, hot-glue the dahlias throughout the arrangement.

*Note:* For instructions on reinforcing stems and clusters with floral wire and floral tape, see "Floral Supplies" on the opposite page.

# FLORAL SUPPLIES

Experienced nature crafters make their lives easier by keeping a few supplies on hand. From picks designed especially for wreath-making to wet and dry floral foam for floral arrangements, these supplies are widely available from craft-supply stores, florists, and mail-order companies. Wreath bases, perhaps the most important of supplies, are covered in a separate section (see "Bases" on page 15).

## Dry Floral Foam

Dry floral foam is a dry, dense, semi-rigid foam material. Available in preshaped wreath bases and in large blocks, this foam may be cut to any shape or size with a serrated knife. Stem ends, floral picks, and floral pins inserted into the foam are held securely in position by the foam itself.

## Wet Floral Foam

Wet floral foam is similar to dry floral foam but is spongelike and water absorbent. It is usually inserted into vases or other display containers for fresh floral arrangements. Available in large blocks and in preformed shapes, it can easily be cut into different shapes and sizes with a serrated knife and will hold inserted materials with ease. The foam should be watered regularly to keep the foliage and flowers fresh.

Commercial wet floral foam bases usually come with a waterproof backing. If you're using this foam in an arrangement that is not protected within a waterproof container, it's wise to place a piece of glass or acrylic between the backing and the surface upon which it rests or to cover the backing with waterproof plastic.

Most wet floral foam is green in color. If you'd prefer that the foam not show in your completed project, disguise its surface with picked or wired materials.

## Polystyrene Foam

The least expensive wreath bases are those made from white plastic extruded foam, such as Styrofoam. Wrap these bases with sheet moss or ribbon before attaching materials to them, or their color may distract from the effects of your completed wreaths.

## Floral Pins

Also known as floral prongs, these U-shaped pieces of wire (see Figure 1) look like elongated staples and are used to attach materials to straw or foam wreath bases or to floral foam. Position the materials to be fastened on the straw or foam, place the pin with its pointed ends on either side of the materials, and push the pin into the straw or foam at an angle.

*Figure 1*

Floral pins are available from craft-supply stores and florists. They are green or silver in color. Select a shade that will complement the colors of your materials.

## Floral Tape

Floral tape has four purposes: to strengthen the weak stems of small clusters that have been wired to floral picks; to reinforce or lengthen individual stems; to disguise unsightly stems or wires; and to cover wire wreath bases and the pieces of floral wire used to secure and fasten bows. This thin, elastic tape, which is mildly adhesive when stretched, comes in several colors—green and brown are the most popular. A stronger, wider version, sometimes referred to as adhesive floral wrapping tape, is also available.

*Figure 2*

To use floral tape, simply stretch it slightly as you work with it, overlapping the tape slightly and winding it down to conceal the materials underneath (see Figure 2). Floral tape may also be twisted tightly to form an attractive, flexible wire.

For fresh-flower projects and others that may be exposed to water, purchase wet/dry floral tape, which is made to withstand the effects of moisture.

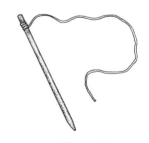

*Figure 3*

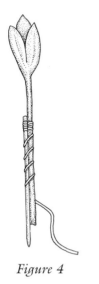

*Figure 4*

*Figure 5*

*Figure 6*

## Floral Picks

A floral pick is a small wooden stick with a taper at one end and a length of fine-gauge wire attached to the other (see Figure 3 on page 115). Usually sold in bundles, the picks are used to strengthen or lengthen fragile stems and to bind clusters of stems together before attaching them to a base or inserting them into an arrangement.

While the stems of some materials are sturdy enough to insert directly into floral foam or straw and foam bases, others are simply too fragile. To test stem strength, insert a stem into a scrap of dry floral foam. If the stem breaks, you'll need to reinforce it with a floral pick, with floral wire, or with both.

### Fastening a Floral Pick to an Individual Stem

First cut the stem to the desired length. Then place the pick next to it, leaving about 1 inch of pick extending past the stem end (see Figure 4). Wrap the wire two or three times around the stem and the top of the pick. Then wrap the wire downward in spiral fashion.

Floral picks differ in thickness; the longer the pick, the thicker and sturdier it will be. To provide extra reinforcement for fragile, short-stemmed materials, select a long, thick pick and whittle it down to the appropriate length before wiring it to the stem.

### Fastening a Floral Pick to a Cluster of Stems

Attach picks to clustered stems just as you would attach them to individual stems (see Figure 5). Because stems vary in thickness, no absolute rule exists regarding the number of stems that can be picked as a single cluster. You're likely to find, however, that a single pick works well with three to five stems. When working with especially delicate stems, you may also need to reinforce the picked stem or stems with floral tape (see Figure 6).

Sometimes, when a cluster of materials is especially large, a single pick may not do the job. What to do? Just attach a second pick for additional support.

### Fastening Picked Materials to Wreath Bases

Picked materials are easy to insert into floral foam, straw and extruded foam bases, and tightly woven vine bases. Take care when inserting picks into floral foam; if you insert the picks too close to one another, your base may disintegrate. (You may need to reinforce a picked item with a dab of hot glue, depending upon its weight and the density of the foam.) To attach picks to loosely woven vine bases, simply hot-glue the picks in place.

## Floral Wire

Floral wire is an indispensable nature-craft supply (see Figure 7). Available in either precut lengths or on spools, this wire comes in brown, green, or silver and in a variety of thicknesses (known as gauges). For use with lightweight materials, select the more flexible fine gauges. When working with heavier materials, less flexible, heavy-gauge wires will provide additional strength.

Precut lengths of floral wire are most often used in conjunction with floral tape to lengthen and strengthen stems and to attach single items to wire and vine wreath bases. When used to attach items to a base, floral wire has one distinct advantage over hot glue: Because you don't have to work quickly when you use the wire, you can experiment with the placement of materials for as long as you like!

### Lengthening and Strengthening Stems with Floral Wire

To lengthen or strengthen a fragile hollow stem, cut a piece of floral wire about 2 inches longer than you'd like the stem to be. Thread the wire firmly but gently through the length of the existing stem and up through the center of the flower. Make a small, U-shaped bend at the top of the wire and then pull it back into the flower so that the hooked end of the wire is hidden (see Figure 8). The wired stem may be inserted directly into a foam or

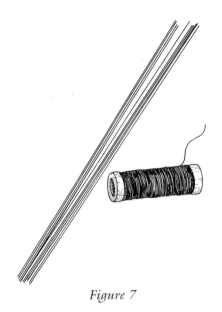

Figure 7

Figure 8

Figure 9

straw base or, if it will be visible in the finished project, wrapped with floral tape before insertion.

Another way to lengthen and strengthen a stem is to reinforce its length with floral wire and floral tape. Cut a length of wire about 2 inches longer than the required stem length. Position the wire along the length of the existing stem and wrap the wire and stem together by spiraling floral tape down their combined lengths (see Figure 9). Trim the wire to the desired length before insertion.

### Attaching Materials with Floral Wire

To fasten stems to a straw wreath base, it's easiest to work with small clusters and a spool of floral wire. Gather the stems together, position them along the wreath base, and attach them to the base by wrapping the floral wire around the base and the stems (see Figure 10). Without cutting the wire from the spool, wire another cluster onto the base so that its blooms overlap the stems of the first cluster. Continue attaching clusters until the wreath base is covered. Don't cut the wire from the spool until you're finished.

Larger items may also be wired to all types of bases, but you may find it necessary to bore small holes in materials, such as dried fruits, in order to string the wire through

the material. (See "Cones, Pods, & Nuts" on page 53 for instructions on how to attach wires to large cones and pods.)

### Floral Tubes

If you'd like to use fresh flowers or foliage in a wreath, garland, or swag, you'll need to purchase clear plastic floral tubes (see Figure 11). Available from florists and craft-supply stores, the tubes are either flat or tapered at one end and have removable caps with small openings in them at the other.

To use a floral tube, first cut the stem of your flower or leaf to a length slightly shorter than the length of the tube. Remove the cap from the tube, fill the tube with water, replace the cap, and insert the stem through the slit in the cap. Floral tubes may be inserted between the strands of loosely woven vine bases. If your base is foam or straw, hot-glue the tube in place. In either case, disguise visible portions of the tubes by covering them with natural materials or with decorative accents, such as bows.

Keep in mind that fresh materials will "drink" the water in the tube within an hour or two. If the tube isn't glued in place, simply remove it to refill it. Hot-glued tubes will need to be refilled while they're still attached. When the flowers and foliage finally wilt, replace them with

Figure 10

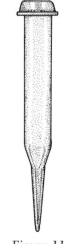

Figure 11

117

fresh materials. Floral tubes are not always watertight, so be careful when you select a location for your finished project.

## Hangers

Nothing is more frustrating to the nature crafter than completing a gorgeous wreath or swag only to realize that there is no mechanism for hanging it. It is so simple to make hangers for your projects that it's a good idea to get in the habit of doing it

as the very first step. You can fashion hangers for wreaths, swags, and garlands by using floral wire or chenille stems (commonly known as pipe cleaners).

To make a hanger for a wreath, form a loop in the center of a 10- or 12-inch length of medium-gauge floral wire or a 12-inch-long chenille stem by twisting it together (see Figure 12). You may want to wrap the floral wire with floral tape first to give the wire a finished appearance. Then wrap the wire or stem around the wreath base and twist the two ends together (see Figure 13). Often, after you hang the wreath, you'll be able to hide the wire by gently curving a flower stem or leaf in front of it.

You can modify this same approach with a swag or garland that has a narrow, horizontal center. You will need several hangers for a long garland. If you want the garland to drape in two or more curves, place a hanger at the peak between every two curves (see Figure 14). If your swag is vertical, you can make the hanger as you construct the swag. When you wire the stems of the flowers or foliage together with medium-gauge floral wire, leave an extra 10 inches or so of wire. Fashion the extra length of wire into a loop, twist the wire end around the wire that is wrapping the stems, and trim the excess wire with wire cutters (see Figure 15).

If you are using a foam or straw base, you can make a hanger that is mounted on the back of the base and is therefore completely hidden from view. Fashion a loop from a 6-inch length of floral wire by twisting the ends together and trimming the excess wire. Identify the place on the back of the base near the top where you want the hanger to be and pierce the foam or straw with the end of the hanger. Remove the wire loop, place a dab of hot glue on the end of the wire, and reinsert it into the base. Then position a floral pin with its prongs on either side of the hanger and press the pin into the base (see Figure 16).

***For more information on using floral supplies,*** *see "Bases" on page 15 and "Tools" on page 208.*

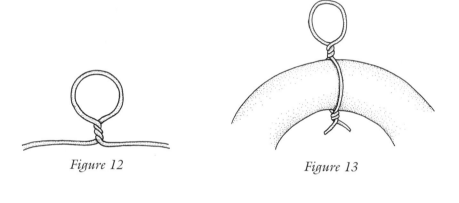
Figure 12

Figure 13

Figure 14

Figure 15

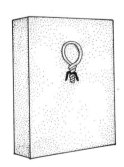
Figure 16

# FRUITS & VEGETABLES

When novice crafters use natural materials, they often limit themselves to flowers and herbs. While these materials are abundant and easily accessible, there are many projects that even urban crafters can make using items purchased from the grocery store. Fruits and vegetables make wonderful arrangements and garlands and are often used as accents in floral projects as well.

It's relatively easy to dry and preserve fruits and vegetables at home (see "Drying" on page 72). But if you'd rather not try your hand at home-drying, look in your local craft shop for dried and fresh materials. Your grocery store is likely to stock a wide variety of miniature pumpkins and gourds during the autumn, and it carries fresh fruits or vegetables year-round. While fresh materials won't last forever, they'll add vibrant color and enliven any arrangement. When selecting fresh materials, always make sure that the materials are as fresh as possible and without blemishes of any kind.

To make fresh fruit and vegetables last longer, pour some acrylic floor wax into an old coffee tin or deep pan. Dip the fruit into the wax, remove it, shake it dry, and drain it on a paper bag. Store the wax, which can be reused many times, in a tightly sealed container. (Do be sure that any children in your household are warned never to eat wax-covered fruit.)

When your arrangement starts to look a little less than fresh, just remove the offending parties and replace them with new ones!

# Fall Fruit & Vegetable Arrangement

*Decorate with an arrangement that's a bit out of the ordinary—fill a basket with fruits and vegetables instead of floral materials.*

## WHAT YOU NEED

1 piece of Spanish moss to fit the basket opening (the opening of the basket shown in the photo is $5\frac{1}{2} \times 11\frac{1}{2}$ inches)

1 fresh red apple

1 fresh pear

1 dried miniature pumpkin

3 garlic bulbs with the stems braided together

3 dried miniature ears of corn

3 dried okra pods, one 8 inches long and two $5\frac{1}{2}$ inches long

4 dried quince slices

4 stems of dried chili peppers, 3 with 4 or 5 peppers per stem and 1 with 2 peppers per stem

1 dried chili pepper without the stem

1 dried miniature sunflower

Basket, any size

2 sheets of crumpled newspaper

8 inches of heavy-gauge floral wire

## WHAT YOU DO

*1* Have fun! If you'd rather select other fresh fruits and vegetables for this arrangement, go right ahead. Open your refrigerator and grab a variety of fresh items in different shapes, sizes, and colors. Oranges, lemons, artichokes, carrots, and onions all look terrific in an arrangement.

*2* Make a nest in the basket by filling it almost to the top with crumpled newspapers. Then cover the newspapers with moss, tucking in the edges well.

*3* Using the photo as a guide, arrange the heaviest materials—the apple, pear, and pumpkin—at various angles on top of the moss. Anchor the garlic bulbs in place by tucking the braided stems under the moss and the pear.

4 Using the heavy-gauge floral wire, connect two of the ears of corn together at their cob ends, leaving a length of wire protruding to insert into the arrangement. Stick this wire into the moss and newspapers, bending it as necessary to drape one of the ears over the front edge of the basket and the other over the edge toward the basket's back. Insert the third ear of corn behind the apple.

5 Place two pieces of okra—one long and one short—near the back of the basket. Insert the third piece in front of the apple.

6 Position the quince slices throughout the arrangement, placing at least one against the back of the basket and angling the others to add visual depth to the arrangement.

7 Using the photo on the opposite page as a guide, insert the chili-pepper stems and the pepper without a stem randomly around the basket arrangement. Insert the sunflower next to the garlic bulbs.

# Country Hat

## WHAT YOU NEED

23 dried ivy leaves

28 stems of dried chili peppers, 1 pepper per stem

3 garlic bulbs with the stems braided together

1 yard of green paper ribbon, 4 inches wide

Hot-glue gun and glue sticks

Straw hat

*To add a bit of country charm to any wall, decorate a simple straw hat with colorful garden materials.*

## WHAT YOU DO

*1* Tie the paper ribbon into a bow and hot-glue it to the base of the hat. (As you arrange the materials on the hat, remember that this project will look best when it's displayed on a wall.)

*2* Starting on either side of the bow, hot-glue the ivy leaves around the rim. Start by placing the two largest leaves next to the bow, arranging them to angle upward around the edges of the hat. As you work toward the top of the hat, vary the leaf sizes and angles. Visualizing the hat as the face of a clock, when you reach the two and ten o'clock positions, start placing the leaves with their tips pointing straight up.

*3* Set aside two stems of peppers for Step 5. Hot-glue the remaining stems onto the rim, tucking the stems under the ivy leaves and varying the pepper sizes and angles. Again, work up from either side of the bow.

*4* Tuck the braided garlic stems through the bow and hot-glue the braid around the side of the hat so that the bulbs will hang slightly below the bow.

*5* Hot-glue the last two stems of peppers between the hat and the bow.

# Miniature Chili-Pepper Arrangements

### Miniature Chili-Pepper Bottle

## WHAT YOU NEED

1 small piece of Spanish moss

5 sprigs of dried sweet Annie, torn into smaller pieces

9 dried strawflowers

11 dried chili peppers

Small glass bottle or vase, 3 inches tall

2 strands of raffia, 20 inches long

Scissors

2 floral picks

Hot-glue gun and glue sticks

*You won't need a country garden or a closet filled with dried materials to make these fun miniatures!*

## WHAT YOU DO

*1* Fill the bottle or vase with the Spanish moss. Wrap the two strands of raffia around the top of the bottle twice. Tie the ends into a bow. Using the scissors, cut the streamers to the desired lengths.

*2* Gather the sweet Annie pieces into two tiny bundles and wire a floral pick to each one. Insert the picks into the moss. Carefully add hot glue, if necessary, to secure the picks.

*3* Hot-glue the strawflowers throughout the sweet Annie, varying the angles for visual interest.

*4* Hot-glue the chili peppers throughout the arrangement, varying their placement angles.

## Miniature Chili-Pepper Basket

## WHAT YOU NEED

1 small piece of Spanish moss

16 miniature hemlock cones

14 dried chili peppers

3 dried ivy leaves

Hot-glue gun and glue sticks

Miniature basket

## WHAT YOU DO

*1* Hot-glue the moss around the inside and the bottom of the basket. Dab a little hot glue onto the bottom of each cone, and working from the edges of the basket toward its center, arrange the cones to cover the moss.

*2* Starting at the outer edges of the basket, hot-glue some of the peppers into the basket. Then insert the remaining peppers among the cones in the center of the basket.

*3* Hot-glue one ivy leaf in the center of the basket and the other two along the edges of the arrangement.

## Miniature Chili-Pepper Swag

## WHAT YOU NEED

2 stems of dried sage, 7½ inches long

1 stem of dried chili peppers, 6½ inches long, with 6 peppers

1 stem of dried oregano, 4½ inches long

2 strands of raffia, 20 inches long

Scissors

## WHAT YOU DO

*1* Set the sage on a flat surface. Position the stem of chili peppers on top of the sage and the oregano on top of the chili peppers.

*2* Wrap the two strands of raffia around the stems twice, about 1 inch from the stem ends. Tie a bow with the raffia. Using the scissors, cut the raffia streamers to the desired lengths.

*Welcome guests to your kitchen with the sweet-and-pungent aroma of a culinary garland made of sage, garlic, oregano, and other herbs and flowers.*

# Culinary Garland

## WHAT YOU NEED

36 inches of woven sisal or raffia braid

22 stems of dried sage: four 7 inches long, six 6 inches long, two 4 inches long, and ten 4½ inches long

2 stems of dried catnip, 7 inches long

4 stems of dried feverfew, 7 inches long

7 sprigs of miniature baby's-breath: two 5 inches long, two 6 inches long, and three 3½ inches long

2 stems of dried yellow yarrow, 4 inches long

10 stems of dried oregano blossoms, six 4 inches long and four 3 inches long

3 garlic bulbs

2 dried Chinese lantern blossoms

2 stems of dried anise hyssop, 5 inches long

2 dried yellow yarrow heads

6 dried single feverfew blossoms

Hot-glue gun and glue sticks

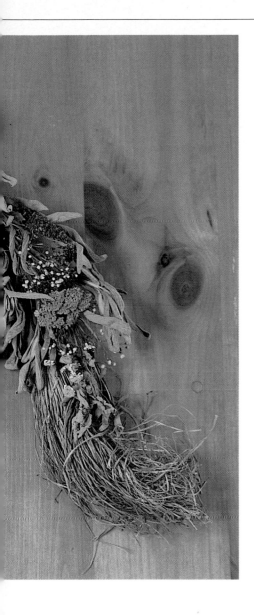

## WHAT YOU DO

*1* Hot-glue one 7-inch-long stem of sage and one 7-inch-long stem of catnip onto each end of the braid so that the tips of the herbs extend down about 2 inches onto the fringe of the braid.

*2* Working from one end toward the middle of the braid, hot-glue the following materials to the braid in this order: one stem of feverfew, one 5-inch-long sprig of baby's-breath, one 4-inch-long stem of yellow yarrow, and one 7-inch-long stem of sage. Repeat from the opposite end of the braid, again working toward the middle.

*3* To each side of the braid, hot-glue three 4-inch-long stems of oregano blossoms and one 6-inch-long stem of baby's-breath. Hot-glue two 6-inch-long stems of sage to each side of the oregano blossoms, then hot-glue one 4-inch-long stem of sage on top of each bunch of baby's-breath.

*4* Continue working toward the center of the braid and hot-glue one garlic bulb to each side. Next, hot-glue one 6-inch-long stem of sage to each garlic bulb and hot-glue one Chinese lantern blossom onto each of these stems of sage.

*5* Hot-glue one 5-inch-long stem of anise hyssop to the outside of each garlic bulb. Hot-glue two 3-inch-long stems of oregano blossoms near the bottom of each Chinese lantern blossom.

*6* Hot-glue one 4½-inch stem of sage below each oregano blossom so that it points toward the inside of the garland. To the outside edge of the oregano blossoms, hot-glue one 4½-inch-long stem of sage. At this point, you should have reached the top of the garland.

*7* Hot-glue two heads of yellow yarrow and one garlic bulb to the center top of the garland, referring to the photograph for placement.

*8* Hot-glue the remaining six 4½-inch-long stems of sage evenly around the center garlic bulb. Just below the center garlic bulb, hot-glue one 3½-inch-long sprig of baby's-breath. To the top center of the garland, hot-glue two 3½-inch-long sprigs of baby's-breath.

*9* To finish the garland, hot-glue three single feverfew blossoms to the top and three more to the bottom of the center garlic bulb.

*Swags aren't just for draping over door and window frames. Experiment with different locations for a stunning effect.*

# Fresh-Flower Garland

## WHAT YOU NEED

60 sprigs of fresh caspia,
6 to 8 inches long

60 stems of fresh asparagus fern,
6 to 8 inches long

8 fresh peach roses

3 fresh white roses

6 fresh Peruvian lilies

10 sprigs of dried dark pink pepperberries, 6 inches long

5 feet of heavy-gauge floral wire

Green floral tape

Spool of fine-gauge floral wire

Cool-melt glue gun and glue sticks

10 yards of gold mesh wired ribbon,
2 inches wide

## WHAT YOU DO

*1* To make the spine for the garland, wrap the 5-foot length of the heavy-gauge floral wire with the green floral tape.

*2* Assemble a cluster of three sprigs of caspia and three sprigs of asparagus fern of various lengths. As described in the "Continuous Garland" method on page 124, wire the cluster to the taped spine with the fine-gauge floral wire. Keep adding clusters of caspia and fern, covering the stems of each cluster with the foliage of the following cluster until you cover the entire spine.

*3* Cool-glue four of the peach roses to the center of the garland. Then cool-glue two peach roses evenly on each side of the garland. Cool-glue one white rose in the center of the four peach roses, and one white rose on each side of the garland. Using cool glue, attach one Peruvian lily to each end of the garland and cool-glue the four remaining lilies in a pleasing arrangement elsewhere on the garland.

*4* Starting at one end of the garland, use pieces of the fine-gauge floral wire to attach the ribbon to the garland. Loop the ribbon over, in front of, and behind the clusters of roses and lilies; wherever the ribbon loops, you will need to wire it to the base. To add bright splashes of color, cool-glue the sprigs of pepperberries alongside the roses and the lilies.

# Rose Garland

*Highlight the colors and patterns of wallpaper trim or other home decor with a glamorous garland.*

## WHAT YOU NEED

92 bundles of dried sweet Annie, 4 to 6 inches long, with about 8 stems per bundle

46 bundles of dried berried eucalyptus, 4 to 6 inches long, with about 4 stems per bundle

23 bundles of dried, light blue larkspur, 4 to 6 inches long, with about 5 stems per bundle

23 bundles of dried, dark blue larkspur, 4 to 6 inches long, with about 5 stems per bundle

36 sprigs of glycerin-preserved juniper, 4 to 6 inches long*

10 large dried pink and/or peach roses

20 small dried pink and/or peach roses

16 dried pink peonies

5 stems of dried hydrangea

15 stems of glycerin-preserved olives, 4 to 6 inches long*

3 large handfuls of Spanish moss

9 feet of heavy, flat electrical wire

Sharp knife

Green floral tape

Black marker

3 green chenille stems, 12 inches long

Hot-glue gun and glue sticks

6 yards of pink upholstery cording, 1 inch wide

Ruler

Spool of medium-gauge floral wire

3 pink tassels

*You can purchase glycerin-preserved materials from craft-supply stores and mail-order suppliers, or you can preserve the materials yourself (see "Preserving with Glycerin" on page 78 and "Preserving Leaves" on page 165).

# Preparing the Gourd

## WHAT YOU NEED

Hard-shell gourd, cured

Plastic dishpan or tub

Dishwashing liquid

Water

Plastic pot scrubber

Sharp, pointed knife

Fine-toothed saw

Black marker or pencil

Steel scraping tool, like a file or rasp (optional)

Sandpaper

## WHAT YOU DO

*1* In the plastic dishpan or tub, soak the gourd in warm, soapy water for 20 minutes and use the pot scrubber to remove all the dirt and mold. Use the back side of the sharp knife to remove tough spots from the skin. Let the gourd dry completely.

*2* Carefully use the fine-toothed saw to cut off the top of the gourd.

*3* With the black marker or pencil, outline the opening you want. Cut through the gourd with the knife and remove the unwanted section.

*4* Remove all the pulp and seeds from inside the gourd; a steel scraping tool can be very helpful. Use sandpaper to shape and smooth the opening and to smooth the inside of the gourd.

# Painted Gourd with Beads

*You can achieve many effects on gourds by using simple dyes and a few carefully chosen embellishments.*

## WHAT YOU NEED

Hard-shell gourd, cured

16 pieces of palm inflorescence (available from basket-supply outlets)

Leather dyes in oxblood and black

Paintbrushes

Acrylic varnish

Electric drill with 1/16-inch drill bit

Compass with pencil

1/2 × 6 × 6-inch piece of wood

Hammer

16 finishing nails, 3 inches long

Spool of fine-gauge floral wire

Wire cutters

Large-eyed needle

Spool of artificial leather sinew

33 red glass beads

7 horn beads

## WHAT YOU DO

1 Complete Steps 1 through 5 in "Preparing the Gourd" on page 132.

2 Dye the gourd with the black leather dye, using a paintbrush or the dauber that comes with the dye. When dry (about 24 hours), dye the gourd with the oxblood leather dye; these dyes are slightly transparent and the black will show through the red to create an attractive and unpredictable pattern. When dry (about 24 hours), apply a coat of the varnish and allow the gourd to dry overnight.

3 Drill a row of holes around the opening, approximately 5/16 inch from the edge and 1/2 inch apart.

4 Using the compass and pencil, draw a circle on the piece of wood the size of the gourd opening. Draw a second circle 3/16 inch larger in diameter. Hammer the finishing nails around the two circles. Place the

133

pieces of palm inflorescence between the two rows of nails. Then wrap the pieces of inflorescence together with four or five pieces of the fine-gauge floral wire. Remove the inflorescence and place it around the gourd opening. Thread the needle with the sinew, knot the end, and pull the needle through one of the holes from the inside of the gourd to the outside. Whipstitch the inflorescence to the gourd, going through all of the holes on the top of the gourd. Remove the floral wire. Knot the end of the sinew close to the inside of the gourd rim and trim.

*5* To hang the beads, tie four pieces of sinew to the stitching on the rim where you want the beads to be located, leaving enough sinew for stringing the beads. String the beads onto the sinew. After the last bead, tie a knot on each sinew thread.

*The careful, symmetrical carving on this gourd creates the illusion of a woven basket.*

# Carved Basket

## WHAT YOU NEED

Hard-shell gourd, cured

Pencil

Keyhole saw

Sandpaper

Off-white acrylic paint (optional)

Paintbrushes

U-shaped wood chisel

Clean rags

Leather dye in brown

Brown paste-wax shoe polish

## WHAT YOU DO

*1* Complete Step 1 in "Preparing the Gourd" on page 132.

*2* Use the pencil to draw lines to indicate the basket handle. With the keyhole saw, cut away large areas of the gourd to create a basket shape with a handle.

*3* Remove all the pulp and seeds. Sand the cut edges and the inside of the bowl. If the inside surface is discolored, apply a light coat of the off-white paint.

*4* Use the pencil to sketch the basket-weave pattern on the gourd. Carve along these lines with the chisel.

*5* Using a clean rag, wipe brown leather dye over the outside of the gourd. Allow the gourd to dry (about 24 hours). Rub brown paste-wax shoe polish over the entire gourd and buff it with clean rags.

# Gourd with Cut-Out Leaves

## WHAT YOU NEED

Hard-shell gourd, cured

2 or 3 fresh leaves in different sizes

Pencil

Sharp knife

Fine-toothed saw

Sandpaper

Black marker

Acrylic paints in yellow, orange, and brown

Paintbrushes

Polyurethane

*This lovely, decorative gourd brings the golden hues of autumn indoors.*

## WHAT YOU DO

1 Complete Step 1 in "Preparing the Gourd" on page 132.

2 With the pencil, outline where you want to cut off a piece of the gourd for the lid. Use the knife to make an initial opening and then use the fine-toothed saw to cut off the lid.

3 Remove all the pulp and seeds. Sand the cut edges and the inside of the gourd until smooth. Do not sand the cut between the lid and the bottom of the gourd because there you want a close fit.

4 Put the lid back on the gourd. Using the leaves as pattern pieces, create a design on the body of the gourd and on the lid by tracing around the leaves with a pencil. All of the leaf tracings must touch or overlap each other. Make sure that the leaf patterns on the lid cross the cut line between the lid and the body of the gourd; this makes the lid fit more securely. Don't put any leaf patterns on the upper rim (right under the lid) or on the bottom of the gourd. Retrace the leaf patterns with the black marker.

5 Use the sharp knife to cut the gourd all the way through between the leaf patterns, being careful to keep the top rim and bottom edge intact.

6 Paint the leaves on the gourd and allow them to dry for 24 hours. Brush on a coat of polyurethane and allow it to dry.

*Create a sensation this Christmas by decorating your tree with a dazzling array of colorful gourds.*

# Painted Christmas Ornaments

## WHAT YOU NEED

Ornamental gourds, cured

Paintbrush

Acrylic paints in your choice of colors

Pen with gold or silver metallic ink (optional)

Clear enamel spray

Ribbon scraps (optional)

Scissors

Craft glue

Electric drill with ¹⁄₁₆-inch drill bit (optional)

Metal ornament hangers (optional)

Assorted small feathers

## WHAT YOU DO

*1* Complete Step 1 in "Preparing the Gourd" on page 132.

*2* Paint the gourds with the acrylic paints and allow them to dry (about 24 hours). If desired, use a silver or gold metallic pen to draw designs on the dry, painted gourds. Spray the gourds with the clear enamel and let them dry overnight.

*3* Attach your choice of hanger to the gourds. If desired, this can be as simple as cutting a loop of ribbon and gluing it to the top of the gourd, or as "professional" as drilling a hole in the top of the gourd and inserting a purchased ornament hanger.

*4* Next, trim the feathers. Apply a small amount of the glue to the underside of each feather and press it onto the gourd. Allow the glue to dry.

# Gourd Birdhouse

## WHAT YOU NEED

Hard-shell gourd, cured

Compass with pencil

Electric drill with $\frac{5}{16}$-inch drill bit

Flexible shaft grinder with a cylindrical-
   shape carbide burr

2 feet of string

Vacuum cleaner

Coat hanger (optional)

Pencil

Acrylic paints in dark forest green, medium dark green, light green, white,
   ivory, yellow, rose, and mauve

2 × 3-inch natural sponge

#4 round paintbrush

$\frac{1}{4}$-inch-wide paintbrush

#00 liner paintbrush

Polyurethane spray

Leather thong, 2 feet long

## WHAT YOU DO

*1* Complete Step 1 in "Preparing the Gourd" on page 132.

*2* Study the gourd to determine where you want to cut the bird's "front door." To make the hole, set the radius of the compass to $\frac{3}{4}$ inch and draw a circle $1\frac{1}{2}$ inches in diameter. Drill a $\frac{5}{16}$-inch hole in the center of the circle and then grind out the hole with the shaft grinder.

*3* To make the holes for the leather thong hanger, drill two $\frac{5}{16}$-inch holes about 1 inch down from the top of the gourd. (You may need someone to hold the gourd steady for you while you drill.)

*4* Place the string through the two thong holes to hold the gourd temporarily. Examine the bottom of the gourd to find the lowest spot for the first of five drainage holes. Mark that spot with a pencil and then mark four more low locations in a cir-

cle around the first hole. Drill five $\frac{5}{16}$-inch holes through the bottom of the gourd.

*5* Using a vacuum cleaner and whatever tools you have on hand (a piece of coat hanger is helpful), completely clean out the seeds and the pulp through the bird's "front door."

*6* Using the photograph as a guide, pencil on your floral design. Lightly sponge all three colors of green paint on the entire area where the floral design will

*Invite wrens, nuthatches, or chickadees to your neighborhood by fashioning this pretty gourd birdhouse.*

# Gourd Jewelry

## WHAT YOU NEED

Cured, cleaned gourd scraps of various shapes and sizes

Pencil

Motorized cutting tool

Sandpaper

Backs and fittings for earrings, pins, and barrettes

Wood-burning tool

Wood glue

Polyurethane spray

## WHAT YOU DO

1 Pencil in the shape of your jewelry piece on the gourd scrap and cut out the pieces with the motorized cutting tool. Sand the backs of the pieces. If you are making a barrette, you will need to make a groove with the cutting tool for the metal-clip backing.

2 On the front of the piece, sketch on and engrave the design with the wood-burning tool. Turn the piece over and glue on the jewelry backs. Allow the pieces to dry for 24 hours.

3 Paint the jewelry, allow it to dry, and spray it with polyurethane.

*The gourd bits and pieces that are left from other gourd projects can be made into attractive earrings, pins, and barrettes.*

*Simple, carved motifs
and subtle coloring
give these gourds a
distinctive and
classic style.*

# Engraved Autumnal Gourds

## WHAT YOU NEED
(for 1 gourd)

Hard-shelled gourd, cured

Pencil

Latex or acrylic paints in your choice
of colors

Paintbrushes

Other coloring agents, such as water
colors, leather dyes, marking pens,
or pastel crayons

Motorized cutting tool with
engraving burr

Clear enamel spray

## WHAT YOU DO

1 Complete Step 1 in "Preparing the
Gourd" on page 132. For the open
gourd, continue through Step 5.

2 With the pencil, draw the decorative
shapes you want, using the photograph
as a guide. Keep it simple. Painting and
carving tiny areas will make this a more
difficult and time-consuming project.

3 Using the paints, dyes, marking pens,
or pastel crayons, color in the areas of
your design. You don't need to color all
the way to the edges of the penciled areas
because the lines will be carved away.

4 With the motorized cutting tool,
lightly engrave along the pencil lines.

5 Spray the finished gourd with several
coats of clear enamel, letting each
coat dry completely before applying the
next one. This is especially important if
you have used nonpermanent coloring
agents, like water colors or markers.

# GRAINS & GRASSES

You don't have to live near fields shimmering with golden wheat to enjoy working with grains and grasses. A few handfuls of fescue from your own backyard and a few more grasses collected from any roadside will provide wonderful materials for your nature crafts—materials rich in texture and available in a surprising range of colors.

Our ancestors certainly knew a good nature-craft material when they saw one. Before the invention of the threshing machine, farmers throughout Europe used stems of wheat and other grains to weave a variety of harvest-related figures and decorative items.

# Grain & Grass Arrangement

## WHAT YOU NEED

3 dried teasel pods, with stems 10 to 16 inches long

Several handfuls of Spanish moss

30 stalks of dried oats, 7 to 12 inches long

80 wheat straws, 7 to 12 inches long

70 stalks of dried rye, 7 to 12 inches long

24 stems of dried Johnson grass, 10 to 18 inches long

24 stems of dried fescue grass, 10 to 18 inches long

12 stems of dried cloud grass, 10 to 18 inches long

12 stems of dried penstemon with seed heads, 10 to 18 inches long

60 stems of dried foxtail grass, 10 to 18 inches long

24 stems of assorted dried roadside weeds, 10 to 18 inches long

30 dried iris pods, with stems 10 to 17 inches long

7 dried columbine pods, with stems 10 to 16 inches long

4 to 8 Japanese black-pine cones

7 stems of dried bunny-tail grass, 10 to 15 inches long

Liquid household bleach

Serrated knife

1 block of dry floral foam

Mushroom container, 6 × 15 inches

Floral pins

Spool of medium-gauge floral wire

Wire cutters

Green floral tape

Electric drill with $\frac{1}{16}$-inch drill bit

Hot-glue gun and glue sticks

*The lush arrangement shown here was designed to be viewed from any side. Don't worry if you're short on materials or can't find the ones listed in the project instructions. Just use a smaller container, adapt the instructions to create an arrangement that will be viewed from one side only, or substitute roadside grasses and grains.*

## WHAT YOU DO

*1* Mix a solution of one part household bleach and four parts water. Place the teasel pods and stems into the solution and allow them to soak until the teasel whitens. This may take from 30 to 60 minutes. Allow the pods and stems to dry.

*2* Using the serrated knife, cut the dry floral foam to fit snugly inside the mushroom container; the foam should stand about 1½ to 2 inches above the container's rim. Cover the visible surface of the floral foam with Spanish moss, securing the moss with several floral pins.

*3* If you find that any of the grass or grain stems are too fragile, strengthen them with medium-gauge

floral wire and floral tape before proceeding (see "Floral Wire" on page 116). Next, sort the oats into clusters of three to five stalks each. Insert these clusters into the foam first, placing the longest ones so that they stretch from one side to the other across the middle of the container. Place the shorter clusters toward the front and back of the container. Be sure that the stalks are secure in the floral foam; each cluster should be inserted 1 to 2 inches deep.

*4* Sort the wheat straws and stalks of rye into small and large clusters. Reinforce the larger clusters with medium-gauge floral wire and floral tape. Then insert the stems throughout the arrangement to create a feeling of density.

# H HERBS

The only difficult aspect of working with herbs is coming up with a common definition for them! We've escaped this dilemma by borrowing this one: Herbs are plants that have been used historically for medicinal or culinary purposes or for their fragrance.

In recent years herbs have jumped from the salad bowl straight into the world of nature crafts. Designers throughout the country have found that these humble plants, which used to be thought of as spindly, small-bloomed, roadside weeds, are not only easy to grow, but are also perfect for making a wide range of projects—from fragrant kitchen projects, like aromatic hot pads, to decorative arrangements and wreaths. The range of colors and textures that they offer is quite astounding, as you'll see when you begin the projects in this section. In addition, many herbs are remarkably aromatic, even after they've been dried; the essential oils in their foliage contribute wonderful fragrances to decorative herbal wreaths and arrangements. Instructions for drying your own herbs are included in "Drying" on page 72.

Most herb plants will thrive even if your approach to gardening is one of benign neglect! All you'll need to grow your own are plenty of sunlight and a patch of garden soil. Herbs even do well in containers, so don't think that if you live in a city, you can't grow them. You'll also find that some herbs, such as goldenrod, grow plentifully in the wild and can be gathered freely. If you're not a gardener or gatherer, dried herbs are available from mail-order suppliers. Don't forget to check your Yellow Pages for local herb farms, too, because these are likely to offer both fresh and dried herbs as well as herb plants for the garden.

In the chart that follows, you'll find descriptions of herbs commonly used in craft projects.

# Herbs for Crafting

| COMMON NAME | LATIN NAME | GROWTH HABITS | PARTS USED |
| --- | --- | --- | --- |
| Anise hyssop | *Agastache Foeniculum* | Tender perennial; 2 to 4 feet in height; prefers partial sun and well-drained soil | (Decorative) Lavender flower spikes; seed heads<br>(Culinary) Blooms |
| Artemisia, 'Silver King' | *Artemisia ludoviciana* var. *albula* | Perennial; averages 3 feet in height; prefers full sun and well-drained soil | (Decorative) Leaves |
| Bay, sweet | *Laurus nobilis* | Tender perennial; up to 12 feet in height; prefers full sun and well-drained soil | (Decorative) Blooms and leaves<br>(Culinary) Leaves |
| Bee balm | *Monarda didyma* | Perennial; 2 to 3 feet in height; prefers full sun to partial shade and well-drained soil | (Decorative) Blooms; leaves; seed heads<br>(Culinary) Blooms |
| Feverfew | *Chrysanthemum parthenium* | Self-sowing biennial; 1 to 2 feet in height; prefers full to partial sun and well-drained soil | (Decorative) Fragrant white flowers with yellow centers |
| Globe thistle | *Echinops* spp. | Perennial; 5 to 7 feet in height; grows under almost any conditions | (Decorative) Round, spiky, azure-colored blooms; leaves |
| Goldenrod | *Solidago* spp. | Perennial; varies widely in height; prefers full sun and well-drained soil | (Decorative) Blooms and leaves |
| Lavender | *Lavandula* spp. | Shrubby perennial; varies in height; prefers full sun and well-drained soil | (Decorative) Blooms and leaves<br>(Culinary) Blooms |
| Lavender Cotton | *Santolina Chamaecyparissus* | Perennial; up to 2 feet in height; prefers full sun and well-drained soil | (Decorative) Blooms |
| Lemon balm | *Melissa officinalis* | Hardy perennial; 1 to 3 feet in height; prefers full sun to partial shade and well-drained soil | (Decorative) Blooms and fragrant leaves<br>(Culinary) Leaves |

*(continued on next page)*

## Nutmeg Grater

### WHAT YOU NEED

3 dried bay leaves

3 dried sage leaves

6 stems of dried lavender cotton, 2 inches long

4 dried chili peppers

2 sprigs of miniature baby's-breath, 2 inches long

2 stems of dried apricot globe amaranth, 1½ inches long

3 whole nutmegs

3 dried feverfew blooms

Nutmeg grater

Hot-glue gun and glue sticks

23 inches of jute cord

4 inches of jute cord

### WHAT YOU DO

*1* Using the photograph on page 157 as a guide, hot-glue the bay leaves to the upper, inside back of the grater. Then hot-glue one sage leaf onto each bay leaf.

*2* Hot-glue three stems of lavender cotton to each side of the inside back of the grater. Then hot-glue two chili peppers at each side.

*3* Hot-glue one sprig of miniature baby's-breath, one stem of apricot globe amaranth, and one whole nutmeg at each side. Hot-glue the remaining nutmeg in the middle of the arrangement.

*4* Make a simple bow with the 23-inch length of jute cord, tying it together in its center with the shorter piece of cord. Hot-glue the bow to the top of the grater, behind the nutmegs.

*5* Hot-glue the three feverfew blooms to the center of the bow.

# Artemisia Tree

### WHAT YOU NEED

120 stems of dried baby's-breath, 18 inches long

150 stems of dried 'Silver King' artemisia, at least 12 inches long

35 dried burgundy or deep pink strawflowers

25 dried love-in-a-mist seedpods

Acrylic spray paint in burgundy

Dry floral foam, 3 × 4 × 12 inches

*Here's one Christmas arrangement that you won't have to dismantle after the holidays! Its beautiful design is perfectly suited for year-round display.*

Cool-melt glue gun and glue sticks

Green wet/dry floral tape

6-inch-diameter shallow bowl

Pruning shears

60 yards of burgundy satin ribbon, ¼ inch wide

Scissors

10 to 12 gray chenille stems, 12 inches long

Wire cutters

Stapler

Floral fixative spray

## WHAT YOU DO

**1** Spray the stems of baby's-breath with burgundy paint and set them aside to dry.

**2** Using the cool-melt glue gun, glue one short end of the foam into the bowl. To further secure it, wrap two to four pieces of wet/dry floral tape from the outer surface of the bowl, up and over the block of foam, and down to the other side of the bowl's outer surface (see Figure 1). Then secure the ends of the tape by wrapping a piece of floral tape around the outer circumference of the bowl.

**3** Choose one flat side of the foam to be the front of your arrangement. To form the basic tree shape, insert some of the artemisia stems with the largest flower heads into the sides and upper surface of the foam, placing them about ½ inch deep and cutting each stem to length as necessary. To establish the peak of the tree, insert one 7-inch-long stem with a very full flower head into the top center of the foam block. The stems at the very bottom of the tree should just touch the worktable surface, thereby ensuring that the bowl will be hidden (see Figure 2).

**4** Once you've established the basic tree shape, use the remaining artemisia stems to fill in the rest of the tree, taking care to make sure that the arrangement is narrower at the top. Vary the angles at which you insert the stems in order to create a natural look. Cut each stem to length as you work. Take your time filling in all the blank spaces and occasionally step back to make sure that the arrangement is taking on the correct shape. Make sure that no foam is visible when you are finished.

**5** The artemisia tree shown in the photograph on the opposite page boasts 24 ten-loop bows. (See "Bows" on page 46 for instructions on making these.) Make the loops about 2½ inches long. To secure each bow, cut a short length of chenille stem and twist it tightly around the bow's center loop; use the wire cutters to trim the wire ends. Cut a piece of ribbon just long enough to wrap around the twisted chenille stem and tie it at the back of the bow. To make tails for each bow, staple together four 5-inch-long pieces of ribbon in a stack. Cool-glue the tails onto the tree first, staggering them so they don't overlap each other. Then cool-glue the bows over the visible staples in the tails.

**6** Cut the spray-painted baby's-breath into springs, and sort them into several small clusters, each about 2 inches wide. Cool-glue the stems of each cluster together. Then cool-glue the clusters into the tree by lifting up the artemisia, inserting each cluster, and holding it in place until the glue sets. Avoid the temptation to add too many of these small clusters; your completed tree will look better if the color contrast between the artemisia and baby's-breath is pronounced.

**7** Cool-glue the strawflowers into the tree, placing them randomly throughout the design. Then cool-glue the love-in-a-mist seedpods in place.

**8** Spray the completed arrangement with the floral fixative. The tree will last for several seasons. To store it, place it in a large paper bag and cover that bag with another paper bag. Store the tree in a dry, dark environment at all times.

*Figure 1*

*Figure 2*

*Clay pots—inexpensive and widely available— serve as attractive bases for these small herbal arrangements.*

# Upsy Daisy

## WHAT YOU NEED

1 piece of sheet moss, 4 inches square

2 wheat straws, 7 to 8 inches long

3 stems of dried anise hyssop, 5 to 6 inches long

1 stem of dried mountain mint, 6 inches long

2 sprigs of miniature baby's-breath, 6 inches long

1 dried pink tea rose on a 4-inch stem

1 dried pink tea rose on a 2½-inch stem

1 stem of dried feverfew, 3 inches long

1 dried yellow yarrow flower head

1 sprig of dried pink pepperberries, 2½ inches long

4 hemlock cones, ¾ inch long

3-inch-diameter clay pot

Hot-glue gun and glue sticks

Dry floral foam, 1 × 1 × 1 inch

## WHAT YOU DO

*1* Turn the clay pot upside down, as shown at left in the photograph, and hot-glue the cube of foam to its bottom. Hot-glue the sheet moss over the foam, allowing it to extend down the sides of the clay pot.

*2* Starting at the back of the arrangement, insert the two wheat straws into the foam. Toward the left of the wheat and just in front of it, insert the stems of anise hyssop, placing the tallest stem in the center. Insert the stems of mountain mint next, in front of the anise hyssop.

*3* Insert the sprigs of miniature baby's-breath on either side of the mint and insert the 4-inch-long rose stem toward the left. Hot-glue the yarrow flower head beside this rose and insert the stem of feverfew in front of the rose.

*4* Place the other rose stem below and to the right side of the yarrow. Hot-glue the pepperberries in the front and center of the arrangement, draping them down over the moss.

*5* Hot-glue two hemlock cones to the left and above the pepperberries. Then hot-glue one remaining cone next to the shorter rose stem and the last cone toward the bottom of the pepperberries.

# Small Garden Spot

## What You Need

1 piece of sheet moss, 2 × 6 inches

2 pieces of dried lichen, 1 × 2 inches

4 stems of dried 'Silver King' artemisia,
8 inches long

4 stems of dried blue salvia, 6 inches long

20 stems of dried lavender cotton,
6 inches long

1 stem of dried pink larkspur,
8 inches long

3 stems of dried anise hyssop,
3 to 5 inches long

1 stem of dried oregano, 4 inches long

1 sprig of baby's-breath, 5 inches long

3 dried love-in-a-mist seedpods,
with stems 3 inches long

1 dried yellow yarrow flower head

2 sprigs of miniature baby's-breath,
3 inches long

1 dried pink tea rose on a 3-inch stem

1 sprig of dried pink pepperberries,
1½ inches long

2 hemlock cones, ¾ inch long

Serrated knife

Dry floral foam, 2 × 2½ × 6 inches

Oval clay planter, 2 × 6 inches

Hot-glue gun and glue sticks

1 artificial bird, 2 inches long

## What You Do

*1* Using the serrated knife, cut the dry floral foam to fit snugly inside the oval clay planter. Hot-glue the sheet moss to the top of the foam, applying hot-glue only around the edges of the foam.

*2* Hot-glue one piece of lichen to the sheet moss at the front of the arrangement and another piece of lichen toward its back.

*3* Insert the stems of artemisia toward the back, left-hand corner, pushing them into the foam so that their heights vary. Then insert the stems of blue salvia in front of the artemisia.

*4* Divide the stems of lavender cotton into two groups and insert one group on each side of the blue salvia. Place the single stem of larkspur in front of the salvia.

*5* On the left side of the arrangement, insert the stems of anise hyssop, locating the tallest in the center. On the right side, insert the stems of oregano and the 5-inch-long sprig of baby's-breath. Then, in the lower left corner, insert the love-in-a-mist, positioning the seedpods to form a triangle.

*6* Directly in front of the larkspur, hot-glue the yarrow flower head in place to fill the hole in the design.

*7* Add one 3-inch-long sprig of miniature baby's-breath to the left of the seedpods and the other to the right side. Then insert the pink tea rose to the right of the yarrow. Hot-glue the pepperberries below the yarrow and the hemlock cones beside the lichen at the front of the arrangement.

*8* Hot-glue the bird to the right of the lichen, as shown at right in the photograph on the opposite page.

*Feel free to substitute any dried herbs for those shown in this arrangement; its structure, textures, and colors are more important than the individual materials used to create the tiered design.*

# Cottage Herb Garden

## WHAT YOU NEED

1 piece of sheet moss, 10 × 24 inches

4 stems of dried 'Silver King' artemisia, 17 inches long

16 stems of dried sweet Annie, 15 inches long

5 stems of dried blue larkspur, 16 inches long

14 stems of dried goldenrod, 15 inches long

4 stems of dried rat-tail statice, 17 inches long

5 stems of dried lemon mint, 14 inches long

10 stems of dried pearly everlasting, 16 inches long

11 stems of dried mountain mint, 12 inches long

8 stems of dried wild oregano or mint, 14 inches long

12 wheat straws, 15 inches long

3 stems of dried sarracenia,* 10 to 15 inches long

6 stems of dried oregano, 6 to 12 inches long

6 stems of dried pink rosebuds on 12-inch stems

10 stems of dried split-leaf mountain mint, 9 inches long

10 stems of dried anise hyssop, 6 to 10 inches long

12 dried love-in-a-mist seedpods, with stems 5 to 10 inches long

8 stems of dried apple mint, 10 inches long

5 stems of dried plumed celosia,
7 to 12 inches long

6 stems of dried cinnamon basil,
10 inches long

3 stems of dried pink larkspur,
11 inches long

8 stems of dried split-leaf mountain mint,
7 inches long

1 dried yellow yarrow flower head

3 stems of dried tansy, 9 inches long

6 stems of dried sage, 5 inches long

4 stems of dried lavender cotton,
7 inches long

4 stems of dried pink yarrow,
5 inches long

2 dried cockscomb flower heads

1 piece of dried lichen, 1½ inches square

2 pieces of moss-covered bark,
1 × 3 inches

2 sprigs of dried pepperberries,
3 inches long

Additional sheet moss (optional)

Serrated knife

1 piece of dry floral foam,
4 × 6 × 17 inches

Wooden crate, 4 × 6 × 17 inches

Hot-glue gun and glue sticks

*Note: Sarracenia is endangered and
should not be collected from the wild.
If you don't grow your own, make sure
that your floral supplier is selling you
propagated, not wild-collected, plants.

## What You Do

1 Using the serrated knife, cut the floral
foam to fit snugly into the crate. Hot-
glue the 10 × 24-inch piece of sheet moss
over the foam to cover it, applying the
glue only at the edges of the foam.

2 Study Figure 1 closely. As you can see,
this arrangement is constructed in

rows. Starting at the
back left-hand corner
of the crate, insert
four stems of 'Silver
King' artemisia into
the foam, followed by
eight stems of sweet
Annie, all of the lark-
spur, eight stems of
goldenrod, all of the
rat-tail statice, eight
more stems of sweet
Annie, and all of the
lemon mint stems.
Finally, in the back
right hand corner,
insert the ten stems
of pearly everlasting.

3 Working now from right to left, insert
the specified numbers of each material
in the next row, as indicated in Figure 1.
Remember that the materials in this row
should be placed slightly lower than those
in the row behind it in order to provide a
tiered effect.

4 Working from left to right this time,
insert the specified numbers of each
material in the third row, again inserting
the materials so that they are slightly
lower than those in the row behind them.

5 To complete the next two rows, first
insert the split-leaf mountain mint,
the yellow yarrow immediately in front of
it, and the tansy next to the mint. Then
insert the sage and lavender cotton in the
front left-hand corner. Next, insert the
pink yarrow in front of the lavender cotton and the crested cockscomb in front of
the apple mint and plumed celosia.
Position the lichen and the pieces of moss-
covered bark toward the center front of
the arrangement. Hot-glue the pink pepperberries on top of the lichen and the
bark so that the berries fill in any open
areas around these pieces.

6 If you wish, hot-glue additional sheet
moss into any cracks in the crate.

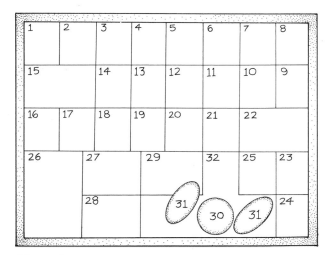

*Figure 1*

1. 'Silver King' artemisia, 4 stems
2. Sweet Annie, 8 stems
3. Blue larkspur, 5 stems
4. Goldenrod, 8 stems
5. Rat-tail statice, 4 stems
6. Sweet Annie, 8 stems
7. Lemon mint, 5 stems
8. Pearly everlasting, 10 stems
9. Mountain mint, 11 stems
10. Wild oregano or mint, 8 stems
11. Wheat, 12 straws
12. Sarracenia, 3 stems
13. Goldenrod, 6 stems
14. Oregano, 6 stems
15. Rosebuds, 6 stems
16. Split-leaf mountain mint,
9 inches long, 10 stems
17. Anise hyssop, 10 stems
18. Love-in-a-mist seedpods, 12
19. Apple mint, 8 stems
20. Plumed celosia, 5 stems
21. Basil, 6 stems
22. Pink larkspur, 3 stems
23. Split-leaf mountain mint,
7 inches long, 8 stems
24. Yellow yarrow, 1 flower head
25. Tansy, 3 stems
26. Sage, 6 stems
27. Lavender cotton, 4 stems
28. Pink yarrow, 4 stems
29. Cockscomb, 2 flower heads
30. Lichen, 1 piece
31. Bark, 2 pieces
32. Pepperberries, 2 sprigs

For an unusual decorative touch at Christmas or Halloween, craft these "balls o' fire" and bring nature's brilliant colors indoors.

# Autumnal Orb

## WHAT YOU NEED (for 1 orb)

Several handfuls of glycerin-treated autumn leaves*

Scissors

Cool-melt glue gun and glue sticks

3- or 4-inch-diameter rigid polystyrene ball

Several yards of gold metallic thread

Straight pins

*You can purchase glycerin-preserved materials from craft-supply stores and mail-order suppliers, or you can preserve the materials yourself (see "Preserving with Glycerin" on page 78 and "Preserving Leaves" on page 165).

## WHAT YOU DO

1 Trim the stems from the preserved leaves. Then, one by one, cool-glue them onto the polystyrene ball, overlapping them as you glue. (Avoid hot-glue guns for this project because they tend to singe the leaves.) Before cool-gluing the last leaf in place, tie one end of the gold metallic thread to a straight pin and push the pin into the remaining uncovered section of the ball. Then cover the pin by cool-gluing the last leaf in place.

2 Using the photo as a guide, randomly wind the metallic thread around the ball until you achieve your desired effect.

3 Cut the thread, tie it to another straight pin, and anchor the pin to the ball by inserting it under the edge of a leaf. Then cool-glue that leaf edge down.

# Gold-Leaf Topiary

## WHAT YOU NEED

Several handfuls of glycerin-treated ginkgo leaves

1 shaggy-bark acorn cap

1 handful of Spanish moss

Gold acrylic spray paint

Small terra-cotta pot

1 bamboo stake or wooden dowel, ¼ inch in diameter and 9 inches long

1 block of floral foam to fit the pot

Serrated knife

Cool-melt glue gun and glue sticks

Plaster of paris

Scissors

Rigid polystyrene cone, 8 inches high

## WHAT YOU DO

*1* Apply a coat of gold acrylic spray paint to the terra-cotta pot, the bamboo stake, and the acorn cap. Let the paint dry thoroughly.

*2* Place the floral foam inside the pot, using the serrated knife to cut it to size.

*3* Insert the bamboo stake into the foam, making sure that the stake is upright. Anchor the stake with cool glue.

*4* Mix the plaster of paris according to the manufacturer's directions. Then pour it into the pot to cover the foam and stabilize the bamboo. The plaster will prevent the weight of the finished topiary from tipping over the pot.

*5* Trim the stems from the ginkgo leaves, and beginning at the base of the polystyrene cone, arrange and cool-glue them in place, overlapping them as you work toward the top of the cone.

*6* When the cone is covered, position it over the bamboo stake and gently push it down to the desired height. Remove the cone, insert

some cool glue into the cavity that you've just created, and replace the cone on the bamboo.

*7* At the very top of the cone, fold over the ends of the leaves so that they lie flat; then cool-glue the acorn cap in place on top of the leaves.

*8* Cover the exposed plaster of paris with the Spanish moss, cool-gluing it in place and trimming the moss as needed.

*Although many nature crafts complement a rustic interior, this gold-leaf topiary is designed for the most elegant room in your house.*

# MOSSES, LICHENS & FUNGI

Some of the most versatile natural materials are also the most humble: The moss, lichen, and fungus that you pay little attention to when enjoying the outdoors can be used to beautiful and practical effect in a wide range of craft projects.

Of the three, moss has the greatest appeal and the most versatility. The most commonly used mosses for floral projects are Spanish, sphagnum, sheet, and mood moss. Moss is used as a wrapping for straw or foam wreath bases and as a base by itself (see "Bases" on page 15). To cover a foam or straw base with Spanish moss, simply arrange the moss around the top and sides and then secure it in place with floral pins or with loose wraps of monofilament or thin-gauge floral wire. If you're using sheet or mood moss, simply wrap it around the base and secure it with floral pins. Sheet moss is often used to cover a topiary form, and sphagnum moss is used for filling the topiary frame. You can also cover other objects: A plain wooden box can be transformed by gluing on a thin layer of sheet or mood moss and then hot-gluing dried flowers to the moss.

Moss is appreciated because it provides a good surface for hot glue to adhere to, and it is receptive to floral picks and single stems of flowers or greenery. When wet, moss retains moisture for days, making it ideal for filling live topiaries. For a natural look, moss stands up well when portions of it are left unadorned. As a decorative touch, moss can be the visual link that pulls together the whole floral design. It adds texture, enhances the natural look of a project, and is an attractive, inexpensive addition on large wreaths, reducing the overall cost of

often pricey purchased materials. Spanish moss makes a terrific filler, too, hiding any gaps that remain between your materials. If the gaps are small, you can simply tuck small clumps of moss into the spaces. With large spaces, you'll need to hot-glue the moss to the base; be sure to use a pencil to press the moss into the glue so you don't burn yourself.

## Harvesting Moss

Moss can be gathered at any time of the year and is usually found growing in humid, shady areas. Collect the moss while it is moist, but be careful—it easily breaks apart when wet. You may need to use a knife to sever the moss from its growth under the top layer of soil.

When you return home, clean off the dirt, sticks, and debris. Place the moss upside down on sheets of absorbent paper and let it air-dry for a week or two. You may need to change the damp paper once or twice. If you follow this process, the moss will retain most of its original color. Kept in a box away from light, the moss will last a long time. If you want the moss to be fresh again, simply wet it.

If you plan to harvest your own moss, please find out which types, if any, are endangered in your area. Even if none are, it's still good practice to take only a small amount from any one locale so that you don't harm the ecosystem. You can also purchase several varieties of moss from craft-supply stores or mail-order suppliers; mail-order companies assert that they grow their own moss and never sell any that are harvested from the wild.

## Using Fungi and Lichens

Fungi and lichens work wonders when used as accents. They mix well with flowers and foliage, providing interesting texture and movement to a floral project. Some varieties look like lace; others look like fossils. When combined with mosses, they give the project a "touch me" quality and a faint, mulch-like aroma of the deep woods.

Most fungi and lichens used in craft projects are gathered from backyards or a walk in the woods; bracket fungi are particularly popular because of their range of color—from white and cream to shades of brown. If you collect your own, allow the fungi and lichens to air-dry for a week or two before using them and store them in covered boxes. Some varieties, such as the sponge mushroom, can be purchased from craft stores or mail-order suppliers. Exercise the same good judgment when collecting these materials from the wild as you do when gathering mosses.

*Decorate a purchased basket or one you've made by assembling an arrangement of treasures from your own backyard.*

# Landscape Basket

## WHAT YOU NEED

Kudzu or grapevine basket,
   7 inches tall and 9 inches in diameter

10 to 12 small rocks

1 piece of mood moss, 12 inches square

1 piece of sheet moss, large enough to
   cover the basket opening

2 pieces of driftwood or 2 sticks,
   3 to 5 inches long

1 stem of dried teasel, 4 inches long

1 stem of dried broomcorn, 4 inches long

5 to 6 small pieces of deerfoot moss

Assorted dried fungi and lichens

*(continued on next page)*

17 to 20 dried bupleurum florets (or any other small, green florets)

2 stems of dried blue larkspur, 4 inches long

7 Australian long-leaf pinecones

3 or 4 small pieces of bark

30 stems of dried tansy, 1 to 4 inches long

6 dried tansy flower heads

4 to 6 stems of dried rose hips, 2 inches long

2 stems of dried quaking grass, 3 inches long

1 small feather

2 or 3 blocks of floral foam, 4 inches square

Sharp knife

Hot-glue gun and glue sticks

Floral pins

## What You Do

*1* Put the rocks in the basket to give it weight. Use enough foam to fill the inside of the basket. With a sharp knife, cut a piece off one block to form a small "hill" and hot-glue it off center toward the back of the basket. Cover this mound with mood moss, using floral pins to secure. Pin the sheet moss on top of the piece of foam in the basket.

*2* To one side of this "hill," add the longer piece of driftwood or a stick, standing it vertically and pushing one end down through the moss into the foam. Place the second piece of wood below the hill, opposite the first piece. To emphasize the height of this hill, add the teasel stem, flanked by the broomcorn, pushing them into the moss-covered foam.

*3* Break the rest of the mood moss into small pieces and wet the piece to make them pliable. Create the effect of a woodland floor by pinning the mood moss on top of the other moss and hot-gluing bits of deerfoot moss into place as accents. Hot-glue the assorted fungi and lichens to the moss-covered foam, with some draped over the edge of the basket and some on the sides. Be sure to turn the basket as you work to make sure you are fully decorating it from all vantage points.

*4* Hot-glue the bupleurum florets in groupings of four to six all over the moss. Hot-glue the larkspur in place. Nestle the pinecones in and around the florets, using hot glue to secure them. Hot-glue the bark in place. Disperse the tansy all over the moss; if the stems are sturdy enough, simply push them into the moss; otherwise, hot-glue them in place. Hot-glue the tansy flower heads onto two sides of the basket. To give a sense of movement, hot-glue the rose hips, the quaking grass, and the feather in a pleasing distribution all over the moss, nestled close to other materials.

# Moss Wreath with Bird

## WHAT YOU NEED

14-inch-diameter straw wreath base

2 pounds of Spanish moss

1 piece of driftwood or a stick, at least 4 inches long

1 piece of sheet moss, 9 inches square

25 pieces of deerfoot moss

Assorted dried lichens, like old man's beard, gray-black lichen, and chartreuse lichen

Assorted dried fungi, found on decaying trees or purchased from suppliers

4 stems of dried yellow yarrow, broken in 12 to 15 pieces

1 martynia pod

2 dried galax leaves

3 dried lemon leaves

3 or 4 dried teasel pods

1 lichen-covered twig, 4 to 5 inches long

Paper from a hornet or wasp nest (optional)

4 or 5 false indigo pods or any dark pod

6 stems of dried tansy, 3 to 4 inches long

18 inches of heavy-gauge wire

Floral pins

Hot-glue gun and glue sticks

1 artificial bird

*Woodland materials are anything but drab when used in an artful arrangement with other natural materials.*

## WHAT YOU DO

*1* Remove the green plastic wrapper from the straw wreath base. With the heavy-gauge wire, fashion a hanger for the wreath as described in "Hangers" on page 118.

*2* Completely cover the wreath base with Spanish moss, using the floral pins to secure. Make sure none of the straw shows.

*3* Attach the driftwood or the stick so that it appears to hang in the center of the wreath. Each piece of wood will be different; its shape will suggest how you need to attach it. For this project, floral pins were hot-glued to the two sides of the wood and then the piece was wedged into the base.

171

*4* Wrap the top third of the wreath base with sheet moss, attached with hot glue and floral pins. Cover the bottom two-thirds with a combination of deerfoot moss and lichens, using hot glue and floral pins. The shell-like lichen on the lower right, as shown in the photograph on page 171, is used to draw your eye away from the bird and back around the wreath. Hot-glue a few bunches of fungi to the base.

*5* Hot-glue the pieces of yarrow to the outer and inner rims and to the top of the wreath. Slip the martynia pod behind some of the moss at the three o'clock position, using a floral pin to hold it to the wreath base. Hot-glue some of the galax and lemon leaves to the base at four o'clock and the rest of the leaves at eleven o'clock.

*6* To vary the height and texture of the wreath, hot-glue the teasel pods near both groups of leaves and the lichen-covered twig at the eleven o'clock position. If desired, hot-glue bits of hornet or wasp-nest paper wherever you notice gaps. To add contrast, hot-glue the false indigo pods to the base at two, four, and ten o'clock. To brighten the wreath, hot-glue the tansy on the lower half of the wreath. To provide a clear focal point, hot-glue the bird to the driftwood.

# Forest Wreath

## WHAT YOU NEED

12-inch-diameter straw wreath base wrapped in birch bark*

2 dried sponge mushrooms

1 small bunch of lace moss

1 large handful of dried black lichen

6 small pieces of moss

8 wild onion bulbs

1 dried globe thistle

3 stems of dried Australian daisy, 1 inch long

24 dried pink globe amaranths

12 dried pink strawflowers

6 stems of dried ornamental grass, 6 inches long

Scissors

Hot-glue gun and glue sticks

*Available at craft-supply stores, or you can make your own by wrapping bark around a straw wreath base and securing it with dabs of hot glue (see "Bark" on page 10).

*Even the most humble materials can work together to achieve an elegant effect.*

## WHAT YOU DO

*1* Hot-glue the sponge mushrooms onto the bottom center of the wreath base, with one in front of the other. You may have to trim the mushrooms with scissors so they will fit the curve of the wreath base.

*2* Hot-glue the lace moss onto the lower half of the wreath base, making sure to cover the inner and outer rims and the front. Hot-glue half of the black lichen onto the lower portion of the wreath base and half between the spaces in the birch bark on the top portion of the wreath base. Hot-glue the small pieces of moss to the bottom half of the wreath base and save one or two pieces to hot-glue to the spaces between the bark, as shown in the photograph on the opposite page.

*3* Hot-glue all the wild onion bulbs directly below the mushrooms. Hot-glue the globe thistle to the left of the front mushroom.

*4* Hot-glue two stems of Australian daisy below the front mushroom and one stem to the left of the globe thistle. Hot-glue all of the globe amaranth and the strawflower heads to the wreath base, clustering most of them below and around the mushrooms to enhance the wreath's focal point. Lastly, hot-glue three stems of ornamental grass on each side of the mushrooms.

# P PAPER

When we think of paper, what often comes to mind is a clean, white sheet of typing or notebook paper—functional and completely without personality. But a sheet of handmade paper might as well be the thumbprint of its designer. As you'll soon discover, handmade paper can be as textured or smooth, as colorful or discreet, and as thick or as thin as you like—and no two sheets will ever look the same.

Making handmade paper requires very few materials—none of them expensive. In addition, papermaking is a craft that invites success. The instructions provided in this section will walk you through the creation of sheet after sheet of beautiful, textured paper that is perfectly suited for making cards, decorative boxes, and fanciful picture frames. Building the simple mold, as described below in "Making the Mold," takes only a few minutes, and the actual papermaking process is so easy that you may want to invite your children to join you. Unless, of course, you'd rather savor the experience alone!

## Making the Mold

On a level work surface, form a rectangle with two pieces of $\frac{3}{4} \times 1\frac{1}{2} \times 11$-inch wood molding and two pieces of $\frac{3}{4} \times 1\frac{1}{2} \times 9$-inch wood molding by placing the shorter pieces against the ends of the longer ones, as shown in the figure on the right. Fasten the pieces of molding together by turning the rectangle on end and by hammering two 8d finishing nails through each short piece and into the end of each longer piece. Then use a staple gun to fasten a $9 \times 11$-inch piece of silk-screen mesh (available at art-supply stores) to the bottom of the wooden rectangle, placing the staples $\frac{1}{2}$ inch apart. For larger molds, just use longer pieces of molding and a larger piece of mesh.

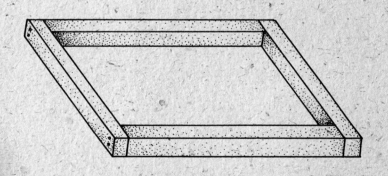

174

# Handmade Paper with Natural Materials

## WHAT YOU NEED (for several sheets)

Several handfuls of dried natural materials, like small blooms, potpourri, leaves, coffee grounds, or tea leaves

Used paper, like newsprint, magazines, or construction paper

Plastic container or bucket

Water

2 pieces of silk-screen mesh, 7½ × 11 inches

Paper mold (see "Making the Mold" on the opposite page)

Blender or food processor

Large, rectangular plastic container, at least 5 × 13 × 15 inches (A new cat-litter pan is ideal!)

Fine-meshed sieve (optional)

1-inch-diameter wooden dowel, 6 inches long

Several cotton towels, pieces of wool blanket, or cotton felt

Large stone or brick with a flat surface

Large sheet of glass or rigid thermoplastic

Paper towels or sheets of blotting paper

Heavy object, like a book or a brick

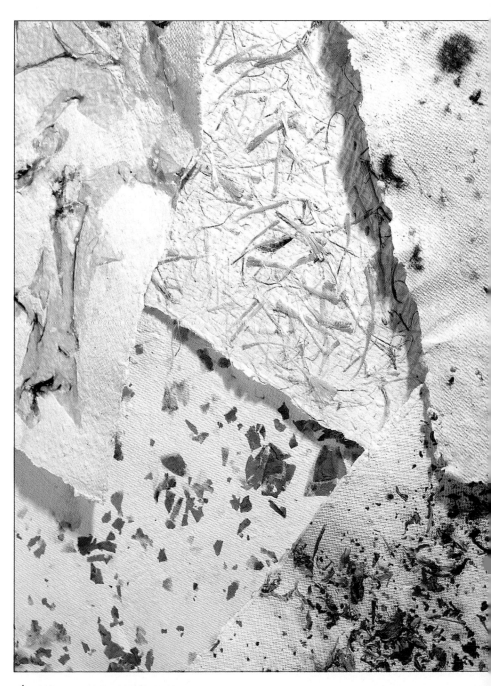

*As autumn nears, capture your summer garden in paper by drying and including a few handfuls of your favorite summer blooms and foliage.*

## WHAT YOU DO

*1* Assemble your materials. Remove all foreign objects from the used paper, including staples and tape. Check to see that the two pieces of silk-screen mesh fit into the mold you've made; they should fit snugly against the bottom without buckling. Set the mold aside.

*2* Cut or tear the paper into small pieces and place them in the plastic container or bucket. Fill the container with water and allow the paper to soak overnight. (If the paper is nonabsorbent, use hot water and allow a few extra hours soaking time.) To make the pulp, fill the blender or food processor two-thirds full with water. Add two or three handfuls of the wet paper pieces. To make the smoothest paper possible, blend the contents until liquefied. For more heavily textured paper, blend only until the paper has been chopped into smaller pieces.

*3* Fill the rectangular container about two-thirds full with a combination of blended pulp and fresh water, adding two cups of pulp to each gallon of water. To make thinner paper, increase the proportion of water; for thicker paper, increase the proportion of pulp. (If you'd prefer to store the pulp and resume work later, press the pulp dry in a fine-meshed sieve and then allow the lump of pressed pulp to air-dry for later use. Resoak the pressed pulp when you're ready to make your paper.)

*4* Sprinkle a handful or two of dried natural materials over the surface of the mixture. Dried flowers and small dried leaves from your garden will add delightful flecks of color. For especially interesting textures, try delicate stalks of dried grasses, seeds, and even common roadside weeds.

5 Place one piece of the silk-screen mesh into the bottom of the mold; it should rest smoothly on top of the mesh that is stapled to the mold. Using one hand, stir the pulpy mixture so that the pulp doesn't sink to the bottom. Then hold the mold by its short ends and dip it vertically into the mixture at the far end of the container.

6 Pull the mold toward you, raising the long bottom edge up as you do; the mold should be horizontal by the time you lift it from the mixture. Papermakers call this step "drawing." Hold the mold in this position, directly over the container, until the water has drained off. The mesh should be covered with an even layer of wet paper pulp.

7 While the newly drawn paper is still in the mold, place the second piece of the silk-screen mesh on top of it.

8 To squeeze additional water from the paper, roll the wooden dowel back and forth several times over the upper sheet of mesh.

*9* Place two or three layers of the cotton towels directly in front of you. Invert the mold over the towels to remove the two screens and the sheet of paper that rests between them.

*10* Place another two layers of cotton towels on top of the sandwiched paper. Then press the flat stone down onto the towels to press out as much water as possible. If necessary, replace the damp towels with dry ones and press again.

*11* Remove the upper layers of cotton towels and the upper piece of screen. Lift the lower screen, with the sheet of paper on top of it, carefully turn it over, and press the paper gently against the glass or thermoplastic drying surface. Rub gently on top of the screen until the paper sticks to the glass. Carefully peel away the screen and rest the sheet of glass or plastic at an angle against a wall.

*12* As the sheet of paper dries, it will pull away from the glass or plastic. As soon as it falls off, place the still-damp sheet flat on a paper towel or blotting paper. Place another paper towel over it and rest a heavy object, such as a book or brick, on top. (When making multiple sheets of paper, stack them for pressing, separating the handmade sheets by covering each one with a paper towel.) You may need to remoisten the paper slightly before pressing it; if it's too dry, it won't flatten sufficiently, even under weights.

*13* Allow the handmade paper to dry for at least 24 hours. To make additional sheets using the soaked pulp, simply begin again with Step 2 on page 176.

# Impressed Papers

A wide variety of natural objects will leave interesting impressions in damp paper. To add impressions to handmade paper, complete Steps 1 through 8 of "Handmade Paper with Natural Materials" on page 175. Remove the upper piece of mesh, arrange your materials on top of the exposed sheet of paper, replace the mesh, and impress the image into the paper by rolling the dowel back and forth over the screen again. Proceed with the remaining steps, but take your time and carefully peel the impressed object from the paper sheet before pressing it against the sheet of glass or plastic.

If you'd like to embed a relatively flat object right into the paper and leave it there, simply insert it between the paper and the screen immediately after the water has been drained from the mold. The unrolled, damp paper will readily accept and retain flat objects, such as leaves and pressed flowers. Proceed with the remaining steps as usual, but do not remove the object from the paper before pressing it against the glass.

*Transforming a sheet of gorgeous handmade paper into a distinctive gift box is a simple matter of cutting, folding, and gluing.*

# Handmade Paper Boxes

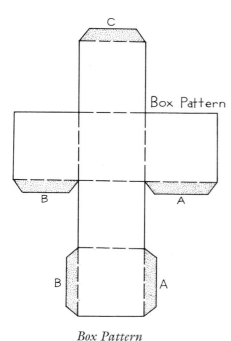

*Box Pattern*

## WHAT YOU NEED

Box pattern

1 sheet of handmade paper
(see "Handmade Paper with
Natural Materials" on page 175)

Pencil

Sharp scissors

Ruler

½-inch-wide paintbrush

Glass of water

White craft glue

## WHAT YOU DO

*1* Have the Box Pattern enlarged at a copy shop until each of the six squares in it is 2¾ inches square. For a larger square box, simply enlarge the pattern as much as you'd like. To make rectangular boxes, draw your own pattern, using the Box Pattern as a guide. Place the enlarged Box Pattern on top of the handmade paper on the surface that will be the interior of the completed box. Use the pencil to trace the pattern's shape onto the paper. Then use the sharp scissors to cut the paper along the exterior pattern lines.

*2* Using the ruler and the pencil, draw in the lines where the paper will be folded. (These appear as dashed lines on the pattern.)

*3* Dry paper will break when folded, so dampen the fold lines by dipping the paintbrush into the glass of water and running the wet brush along each fold line.

*4* Fold the paper to make a box and glue together the sections represented by the shaded portions of the pattern.

*An inexpensive picture frame from your local discount mart makes a fine base for a one-of-a-kind paper covering.*

# Paper-Covered Frames

## WHAT YOU NEED

Several sheets of damp handmade paper (see "Handmade Paper with Natural Materials" on page 175)

1 roll of plastic wrap

2½-inch-wide paintbrush

Picture frame, any size

White craft glue

Small sponge, dampened with water

Clear polyurethane

## WHAT YOU DO

*1* To accumulate sheets of damp paper, complete Steps 1 through 10 of "Handmade Paper with Natural Materials" on page 175 and, as you remove the paper sheet from the mold, press it between towels. Then place the damp sheet on a flat piece of plastic wrap. Cover it with a second sheet of plastic wrap. As you make more sheets, continue to build the stack by layering sheets of paper and plastic wrap.

*2* Use the paintbrush to coat the frame with a layer of the white craft glue.

*3* Using your fingers and a damp sponge, shape the sheets of paper around the frame, carefully tearing them into smaller pieces to make them more manageable. Be sure to overlap the paper at every seam. Pat the paper-wrapped frame with the damp sponge to smooth its surface.

*4* Place the frame in a warm, dry location to dry. As the paper dries, it will shrink and cling tightly to the frame. After the paper-coated frame has dried thoroughly, paint it with one thin coat of clear polyurethane.

## Spice 'n' Apple Potpourri

2 cups of dried chamomile flowers

2 cups of dried sage leaves, cut into pieces

1 cup of dried spearmint leaves,
    cut into pieces

1 cup of dried calendula flowers,
    cut into pieces

¼ cup of anise seeds

2 cups of dried apple pieces

1 cup of dried rose hips

½ cup of dried orrisroot pieces (fixative)

1 teaspoon of natural clove-bud oil

1 tablespoon of synthetic spice 'n' apple oil

## Spicy Vanilla Potpourri

1 cup of star anise

1 cup of cinnamon-stick pieces

½ cup of nutmeg pieces

1 cup of whole cloves

1 cup of sandalwood pieces

2 vanilla beans, cut into pieces

1 cup of dried white globe amaranth

1 cup of dried pink globe amaranth

1 cup of cellulose fiber (fixative)

1 teaspoon of natural vanilla oil

## Fragrant Garden Potpourri

1 cup of dried rose petals

1 cup of dried lavender buds

1 cup of dried orange peel

1 cup of dried rosemary, cut into pieces

½ cup of dried hibiscus blooms,
    cut into pieces

½ cup of whole cloves

½ cup of dried yellow yarrow heads, crumbled

## Forest Fantasy Potpourri

1 cup of dried spruce needles,
  cut into ½-inch lengths

1 cup of dried rose hips

1 cup of dried rosemary needles

1 cup of dried lemon balm, cut into pieces

1 cup of dried bee balm heads,
  broken into pieces

1 cup of dried anise hyssop heads, stripped from stems

1 cup of dried pineapple sage blooms

1 cup of dried pepperberries

1 cup of dried pine needles, cut into
  ½-inch pieces

1 cup of dried white-pine cone petals

Several small sprigs of dried plume fern

½ cup of cellulose fiber (fixative)

20 drops of natural spruce oil

## Fabulous Faux-Strawberry Potpourri

3 cups of dried oak moss, cut into pieces

2 cups of dried everlasting flowers

½ cup of cinnamon-stick pieces

1 cup of dried bay leaves, cut into pieces

1 cup of whole cloves

1 cup of dried rose petals

2 cups of dried 'Strawberry Fields' globe-amaranth
  heads

1 cup of cellulose fiber (fixative)

1 teaspoon of synthetic strawberry oil

1 teaspoon of natural rose-geranium oil

½ teaspoon of natural vanilla oil

*For **additional potpourri projects**, see "Sachets"
on page 194.*

# PRESSED FLOWERS & HERBS

There are many different types of flowers that press well, as indicated in "Flowers, Herbs, and Foliage for Craft Projects" on the opposite page. Look for small flowers with thin plant parts since it's hard to press large, bulky forms and still have them resemble their original appearance. Intricate blossoms or flowers with variegated colors, such as daisies and pansies, lend themselves well to pressing. Some flowers retain their color better than others. Experiment with the flowers you find. You may be surprised at how uncommon the common dandelion can look when it is pressed.

After you have gathered your plant materials, remove the foliage or blooms from the stems. Place each plant flat on a piece of porous paper, such as blotting paper or a paper towel. Arrange each piece into the appearance you want; once the plants dry, you will not be able to change their shape. Play Mother Nature now: Curve some stems, leave others straight, put an arch into others. This way, your pressed flowers will reflect the infinite variety of live, growing plants. Make sure the plants do not touch each other. Cover them with another piece of porous paper. Then put the plants and the papers into a commercial plant press, place them between the pages of a heavy book, or stack books on top of them (see the photograph on the left).

Depending on the thickness and the size of what you are pressing, the plant material can take from several days to nearly a month to dry completely.

When you work with your pressed flowers, make sure the scale of the plants is compatible with the use you envision for them. Try adding a few petals from one flower to embellish a different flower. Create a design with a single stem of blossoms, or break off the blooms and scatter them. Imagine that the pressed flowers are your paints and create a bold and inventive still life.

Pressed flowers, plants, and herbs are delightful materials to use in nature-craft projects, and the pressing process is very simple. Basically you want to dry the plants as flat as possible. You can do this by using a purchased plant press or a heavy book.

Always pick the plants when they are at their best, well before they have peaked. This is true whether you are working with spring flowers or herbs, summer foliage, autumn leaves, or winter blooms.

When pressing plants, the materials must be in top condition so that they will hold up well and keep their shape and color. Pick more materials than you think you will use so that you will have a good selection, and be sure to pick a variety of plants.

*This beautiful notecard was made by gluing pressed pansies to handmade paper with a spray adhesive.*

# Flowers, Herbs, and Foliage for Craft Projects

Spring: carnation, clematis, crocus, ferns, honeysuckle, iris, Johnny-jump-up, morning glory, pansy, phlox (wild blue), primrose, squill, viola, violet, wallflower.

Summer: angelica, bachelor's-button, bay leaf, bee balm blooms, coneflower petals, cosmos, daisy, dandelion, feverfew, flax, geranium, impatiens, ivy, larkspur, lavender, marigold, oregano (blooms and foliage), Queen-Anne's-lace, roses (small flowers and buds), sage blooms, santolina, 'Silver King' and 'Silver Queen' artemisia, tarragon leaves, tickseed (annual), zinnia (single, not double varieties)

Fall: aster, calendula, chrysanthemum (single variety), goldenrod, hydrangea blooms, maple leaves

Winter: Christmas rose, winter jasmine

Pressed flowers add beauty to even the simplest project. To create the note cards on page 192, pansies were glued (just a tiny dab, please) to handmade paper (see "Handmade Paper with Natural Materials" on page 175). To embellish a plastic frame box, glue pressed ferns to the cardboard backing, cover the backing with tissue wrapping paper, and paint the surface with white craft glue. Trim the paper to fit the frame, let it dry, and you have a lovely background for framing any special photograph. The two projects in this section are variations of these easy approaches.

191

*With these easy-to-make note cards, you can capture the fleeting beauty of summer flowers under the illusion of a light wrapping of parchment.*

# Pressed-Flower Note Cards

## WHAT YOU NEED (for 1 card)

5 to 10 assorted pressed flowers

2 pieces of waxed paper, 12 inches square

1 two-ply white facial tissue

Cup or small bowl

Small wooden spoon

White glue mixed half and half with water

Soft camel-hair lacquer brush, 1 inch wide

Brown paper grocery bag

Scissors

Iron

1 sheet of light-colored drawing or writing paper, 8½ × 11 inches or smaller

12 inches of satin ribbon or gold cord, ¼ inch wide

## WHAT YOU DO

*1* Place one piece of the waxed paper flat on your work surface. Arrange the pressed flowers attractively for the front of the card. Be sure that the flower arrangement is either in the center of the bottom half of the paper or in the center of the right-hand half of the paper because you will be folding the paper in half either horizontally or vertically to make the card.

*2* Take one piece of the facial tissue, pull off one ply of the tissue, and place it over the pressed flowers arranged on the waxed paper. Be careful not to move the flowers.

*3* In the cup or small bowl, mix the glue and water with the wooden spoon. With the camel-hair brush, carefully paint the glue mixture over the tissue, the flower arrangement, and the waxed paper. In order not to tear the delicate tissue paper, use small, light strokes and don't go back over any of the tissue. Be sure to paint the entire tissue, even where there are no flowers. The tissue will wrinkle some. When dry (after about 24 hours), the wrinkles will make the paper look like expensive, handmade paper.

*4* Cut a slit down one side of the grocery bag and cut off the bottom of the bag so that you can fold it in half and it will lie flat. Place the other piece of waxed paper between the two layers of brown paper. Iron with a warm iron so that some of the wax will transfer from the waxed paper to the brown paper. Remove the waxed paper from between the folded brown paper. Fold the dry tissue-flower-and-waxed-paper sandwich in half the way the finished card will be folded and place it between the folded brown paper. Again, iron the brown paper. This time, the wax will transfer from the brown paper to the sandwich to give it a smooth finish.

*5* Remove the folded tissue-paper sandwich. Fold the piece of colored drawing or writing paper in half and slip it inside the tissue-paper sandwich. If necessary, trim the tissue paper to fit.

*6* At the center of the card's fold, make two small V-shaped cuts about 1 inch apart. Thread the ribbon or cording through the holes and tie a bow on the outside of the note card.

# Decorated Potpourri Jar Lids

## WHAT YOU NEED (for 1 lid)

3 to 5 assorted pressed flowers

Potpourri (see "Potpourri" on page 187)

1 sheet of white or light-colored paper, 8½ × 11 inches or smaller

Pencil

Glass jar with a lid

Scissors

1 piece of clear self-adhesive vinyl, 10 inches square

White craft glue

12 inches of ribbon or raffia

*Create a welcome gift by dressing up a jar of potpourri with a simple, pressed-flower lid.*

## WHAT YOU DO

1 On the piece of white or light-colored paper, trace around the lid you want to cover. Cut out this circle and arrange the pressed flowers on the paper.

2 Cut out a circle of clear self-adhesive vinyl 1 inch larger in diameter than the jar lid. Peel the backing from the self-adhesive circle and place it, centered, over the pressed flowers on the paper circle. Press the vinyl carefully and thoroughly to make sure it fully adheres to both the paper circle and the flowers.

3 Make a series of cuts around the decorated circle from the edge of the clear vinyl to the edge of the white or light-colored paper. These should look like tabs. Center the decorated circle over the lid and press the tabs around and under the lid to attach the cover to it.

4 Fill the jar with potpourri, and screw the lid back onto the jar. Glue a piece of ribbon or raffia around the rim of the lid, or if the rim of the lid is a color that you like, just tie a ribbon around the neck of the jar.

# S SACHETS

Sachets are small fabric bags filled with a fragrant blend of dried natural materials. Centuries ago, these scented bags often contained specific herbs used for specific purposes—herbs thought to repel insects, to invite sweet dreams, or to protect against the plague, for example. Today, most crafters use sachets simply for the wonderful fragrance that they magically bestow to objects nearby. No matter where a sachet is placed—in a linen closet or lingerie drawer or under an armchair cushion—its fragrance will fill the area.

Long ago the contents of sachets were ground to a fine powder. Today, finely chopped potpourri is used instead. Tightly woven, natural-fiber fabrics, such as cotton, linen, or silk, make the best sachet covers since even the larger bits and pieces that make up contemporary potpourri can leak through loosely woven fabrics.

The sachet project that follows serves a dual purpose. By using a decorative fabric and embellishing it with dried flowers or herbs, whole spices, and ribbons or lace, you'll create a decorative sachet that's worthy of display on an open shelf or guest-bedroom pillow. When made to the specifications given here, however, it also serves as a wonderfully refreshing bath scent.

If you plan to make a decorative sachet and set it on precious upholstery or in a treasured basket, you may want to sew a cotton liner into the sachet bag or place a protective covering inside the basket. Potpourri ingredients may stain if they leak from the bag or get wet. To rejuvenate the fragrance of any sachet, just crush its contents by squeezing the bag or gently tapping it with a tack hammer.

*Hang this sachet under the hot-water tap of your tub or float it in your bath water for a fragrant break from the hustle and bustle of everyday life.*

# Bath Sachet

## WHAT YOU NEED (for 1 sachet)

¾ cup of your favorite potpourri blend, chopped finely (see "Potpourri" on page 187)

1 piece of cotton fabric, 4 × 10 inches

Iron

Sewing machine or needle and thread

Blunt-tipped tapestry needle

12 inches of cotton string

Cotton ball

10 inches of wide yellow ribbon

## WHAT YOU DO

*1* With the wrong side of the fabric facing up, fold up each short edge ⅜ inch and press the folds with the iron (see Figure 1).

*2* Create a casing by stitching each fold with a ¼-inch seam allowance.

*3* With the right sides together, fold the fabric in half crosswise and press. Sew the two unstitched edges closed with a ¼-inch seam allowance (see Figure 2). Turn the bag right side out and press.

*4* To make the drawstring, thread the tapestry needle with the cotton string. Insert the needle into the casing through the seam on one side. Being careful to leave a short thread tail hanging from the casing, run the cotton string through the casing, exiting the casing at the other seam and then entering the opposite casing. Run the thread through that casing and out of the bag (see Figure 3).

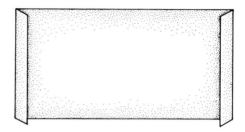

*Figure 1*

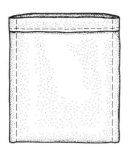

*Figure 2*

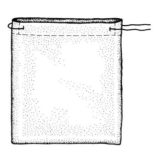

*Figure 3*

*5* Remove the needle and fill the bag with the potpourri. Place the cotton ball on top of the potpourri to keep the ingredients from escaping. Tightly pull the drawstring closed and tie the ends in a double knot to secure the bag's contents.

*6* To make the decorative bow, fold the ribbon in thirds, place it across the drawstring knot and tie it securely with the ends of the string.

*7* Tie the loose ends of the drawstring together to create a loop to serve as a hanger. Hang the bag under the hot-water tap and run your bath water. Before bathing, remove the bag, squeeze it dry, and hang it on a towel rack to dry. The sachet ingredients will last for four or five baths.

## Fast and Easy Sachets

Sachets can be any shape. To make small, decorative versions, use pinking shears to cut a circular piece of fabric, then place a handful of potpourri in its center (see "Potpourri" on page 187 and "Drying" on page 72). Using your fingers, gather the edges of the fabric together and tie the miniature sack closed with an attractive ribbon. Embellish as desired.

## WHAT YOU DO

*1* Assemble the plants and the materials. Use the glass cleaner and the paper towels to clean the aquarium inside and out. Allow the aquarium to dry thoroughly before proceeding.

*3* Pour a 1-inch-thick layer of perlite into the bottom of the aquarium to allow for drainage.

*2* Using the pen or the marker, draw a terrarium "floor plan" on the piece of cardboard, indicating where you want to place each plant as well as the decorative stone. Note that the floor plan in the photograph below and on the right depicts the numbered plants as follows:

| | |
|---|---|
| #1 = Crassula | #5 = Stapelia |
| #2 = Haworthia | #6 = Faucaria |
| #3 = Euphorbia | #7 = Sempervivum |
| #4 = Gasteria | #8 = Sedum |

*4* Position the large stone on the perlite for a natural, decorative effect; use smaller stones, too, if desired. Then add potting soil, sculpting it as desired. Bury at least one-half of the stone as you add the soil, firming it lightly.

*5* Using the cardboard layout as a location guide, excavate holes with the large spoon or your hands. Plant each succulent in turn, firming the soil around the roots. Be careful not to set the plants any deeper than they were in their pots. (To remove a plant from its plastic container, tap the sides of the container gently and run a thin-bladed knife around the inside surfaces. Cradling the plant in your hand, turn the pot upside down and gently remove the pot.)

*6* Use a small, soft paintbrush to remove any dirt from the foliage. Spread plain or colored aquarium gravel in a thin layer over the soil surface, getting it as close as possible to the base of each plant. Substitute sand if you wish.

*7* Using the spray bottle, mist the soil with one to two cups of water, applying it between the plants, not on them. Use paper towels to clean the inside of the glass. (If you've used woodland plants instead of succulents, use an aquarium lid, leaving it slightly cracked to provide fresh air.) Water only when the plants appear shrunken or shriveled or when the soil begins to pull away from the sides of the container.

# TOOLS

As a nature crafter, you won't need a "high-tech" workshop. In fact, your complete tool set will probably fit into a kitchen drawer. What's more, many of these required tools may be lurking in your household already, just waiting to be put to creative use.

For descriptions of craft-specific tools, such as those used in basketry, simply turn to the section in which that craft is described. The tools listed here are the ones you'll need for almost every project in this book.

## Clippers or Pruning Shears

For harvesting your own materials, for cutting stems to length, for snipping sprigs from stems, and for cutting basketry materials, a high-quality pair of garden clippers or pruning shears is a must.

## Glue Guns

Glue guns are to nature crafters what wrenches are to mechanics—absolutely indispensable. These wonderful tools are available at any craft-supply or hardware store and are so useful that you'll wonder why every household doesn't own one. If you've never handled a glue gun before, take time to read the manufacturer's instructions carefully.

The gun-shaped tool, which accepts solid glue cartridges, plugs into any household receptacle. When its trigger is squeezed, a drop of hot liquid glue is released from the gun's conical tip. Available in a variety of sizes, and in hot-glue and cool-melt versions, glue guns are worth every penny of their cost—and they aren't expensive!

Hot-glue guns are especially useful for securing materials such as stemless blooms or small cones and pods; for adding bits of materials to fill in empty spaces in an arrangement; for securing large, light materials, such as slices of dried fruit; and for securing larger, wired items. Unless you're gluing small, last-minute additions to the outer surface of a base or arrangement, don't hesitate to use quite a bit of glue. You'll find that the gun may leave strands of excess glue behind as you work, but these are easily removed once they've dried.

Because hot-glue guns can cause painful burns when handled carelessly and because some materials are easily damaged by extremely hot glue, some crafters also purchase cool-melt glue guns, which make use of a glue that melts at lower temperatures.

## Needle-Nose Pliers and Wire Cutters

Needle-nose pliers and wire cutters will also prove useful in your nature-craft workshop. You will use the wire cutters to cut floral wire to length and the needle-nose pliers to bend the wire into necessary shapes.

## Ruler or Tape Measure

Many of the projects in this book require that stems be cut to certain lengths, so keep an 18-inch-long ruler or a short tape measure on hand. If you have a work surface that you use only for nature crafts, try this trick: Hot-glue a ruler right onto the surface itself. Then all you'll need to do is hold each stem next to the ruler with one hand while you snip the stem with clippers or pruning shears held in the other hand.

## Scissors

Be sure to keep at least one sturdy, sharp pair of scissors on hand. You'll be cutting up a storm as you handle ribbons, slender sprigs of dried materials, corn husks, and many other nature-craft materials and supplies.

# TOPIARIES

Topiary originally referred to the sixteenth century art of training and trimming trees and shrubs into unusual or ornamental shapes. Later, topiary included the shaping of wire into animal forms and other shapes that were filled with moss and then planted with fresh foliage. Contemporary topiary has added yet another variation: A polystyrene ball or cone, skewered on a stick and fastened into a pot, is covered with moss, dried flowers, and other natural materials. This is the topiary art that most of today's designers practice and that has come to be nearly synonymous with the word topiary.

Topiaries can be large or small, simple or extremely ornate, rustic or dressy, and made with fresh, dried, or artificial materials (or artful combinations of all three). What they share is their basic construction. In recent years, topiaries, such as the three projects included here, have become quite popular and offer nature crafters an appealing, easy way to decorate their homes and create welcome gifts.

# Dried-Rose Topiary

## WHAT YOU NEED

¾-inch-diameter green tree branch, as straight as possible and 12 inches long

3-inch-diameter grapevine wreath

1 piece of sheet moss, 12 inches square

5 bunches of dried red roses, 20 to 22 stems per bunch

Pruning shears

Ruler

1 small piece of plywood

Serrated knife

1 block of floral foam, 5 inches square

5-inch-diameter terra-cotta pot, 4 inches tall

Hot-glue gun and glue sticks

5-inch-diameter polystyrene ball

## WHAT YOU DO

*1* Using the pruning shears, ruler, and plywood, cut both ends of the tree branch on a diagonal. Use the serrated knife to cut the floral foam to fit in the terra-cotta pot. Insert the foam into the pot.

*2* Use one end of the branch to make a hole in the center of the floral foam in the pot. Remove the branch, generously cover the end of the branch with hot glue, and insert it back into the block of foam. Hold the branch for two minutes so the glue can set. Using the same process, attach the polystyrene ball to the other end of the branch.

*3* Unwind the small grapevine wreath and clip a 15-inch piece of vine from it. Put hot glue on one end of the vine and insert that end into the foam in the pot, close to the tree branch. Wind the vine up the branch, put hot glue on the free end of the vine, and insert it into the bottom of the polystyrene ball.

*4* Cover the top of the pot with the sheet moss. Then carefully cover the entire ball with the sheet moss, using dabs of hot glue to secure the pieces of moss, making sure that no foam is visible.

*5* Use your fingers to strip all of the leaves from the rose stems and put the leaves aside. Using the pruning shears, trim two-thirds of the rose stems to varying heights, ranging from 1 to 3 inches. Trim a third of the stems right up to the rose.

*6* Assemble clusters of two to three roses with stems of varying heights, and starting at the top of the moss-covered ball, insert the stems through the moss into the ball. Hot-glue the shortest stems and the roses with no stems directly to the moss. Hot-glue two or three of the rose leaves alongside each rose cluster. Continue in this manner until the entire ball is covered. Wherever there are gaps in the ball, fill in with the rose leaves. You may want to put the small clay pot into a larger, decorative pot, add more sheet moss at the foot of the topiary, and hot-glue three or four rose stems to the moss.

*Dress up a front-hall table with this rich, red fruit topiary, which can also serve as a decidedly different Christmas decoration.*

# Pomegranate Topiary

## WHAT YOU NEED

Twig and grapevine topiary base*

1 piece of sheet moss, 8 × 10 inches

8 dried pomegranates

100 acorns or several bunches of artificial grapes

20 pieces of dried hydrangea blooms

Assorted mosses, lichens, and fungi (see "Harvesting Moss" on page 168)

Small bucket

1 pound of plaster of paris

Water

5 or 6 finger-size pieces of damp sponge

Terra-cotta pot or other container slightly larger than the diameter of the grapevine ball

Scissors

Hot-glue gun and glue sticks

Acrylic spray paints in red and black

Clear acrylic spray

Wire cutters

*A twig attached to a grapevine ball can be mail-ordered from suppliers (see "Supply Sources" on page 254) or through your local florist; several sizes are available.

## WHAT YOU DO

1 In the small bucket, mix the plaster of paris with the water according to the instructions on the package. Place the sponge pieces vertically all around the terra-cotta pot on the inside wall and pour in the plaster (the damp sponge pieces will adhere to the pot and keep the pot from cracking as the plaster dries and expands). Insert the topiary-base twig into the center of the plaster, pushing it all the way to the bottom of the pot. Make sure the twig is centered and straight. Hold it for five minutes until the plaster begins to set or prop it up with pieces of dry sponge. Allow the plaster to set (about five days).

2 With the scissors, cut the sheet moss into little pieces and hot-glue them to the grapevine ball, but don't cover the entire ball; much of the charm of this topiary is that the vine shows through.

3 Hot-glue the pomegranates onto the ball in an even but random distribution, checking to see that the placement looks even from all angles.

4 If you are using acorns, treat them as follows: Spray them with red acrylic paint and let them dry. Then stand about two feet away and mist the acorns with black paint to achieve a more cherry color. When they are dry, spray them with the clear acrylic. Allow them to dry and hot-glue them onto the ball. If you are using artificial grapes, simply hot-glue small bunches (use wire cutters to cut the grapes off the main bunch) onto the ball.

5 Fill in the topiary ball with hydrangea blooms, mosses, lichens, and fungi, using hot glue to secure the pieces.

6 Cover the opening of the pot with sheet moss. Decorate the pot by hot-gluing a few lichens and a few grapes or painted acorns to the moss.

# TUSSIE MUSSIES

Tussie mussies are tiny bouquets made with fresh or dried flowers and herbs. Women in Elizabethan England treasured these nosegays not only because they were attractive, but because they served to mask the unpleasant odors associated with everyday life in a country without sanitation.

By Victorian times, many flowers and herbs had acquired symbolic meanings. Tussie mussies of that day were often made with particular plants as a way of conveying messages with flowers. For example, an ardent suitor determined to convince his lady-love of his good intentions might offer her a tussie mussie filled with lavender (devotion), artemisia (constancy), and yarrow (dreams of a loved one). "The Victorian Language of Flowers" chart on page 101 translates just a few words and phrases into "the language of flowers."

Methods for making tussie mussies vary, but you'll find that the two presented here are very similar. In the first project, dried and fresh herbs and flowers are wrapped together, one material at a time. The wrapped stems are then either inserted into a doily cuff or rewrapped with an attractive ribbon. The second and third projects are made by first composing the materials into bunches and then wrapping the bunches together. Additional materials are hot-glued into place once the bouquet has been shaped.

*Using both fresh and dried materials in your tussie mussies allows you to combine the prettiest flowers of the season with the best selections from your local craft-supply store or florist.*

# Fragrant Tussie Mussie

*Bold colors and large zinnia blossoms make this tussie mussie a definite eye-catcher.*

# Zinnia Tussie Mussie

## WHAT YOU NEED

20 stems of dried oregano, 5 inches long

15 stems of dried tansy, 3 inches long

35 stems of dried pennyroyal, 5 inches long

3 medium-large dried hydrangea heads, broken into smaller pieces

6 dried zinnias: one 2½ inches in diameter, three 2 inches in diameter, and two 1½ inches in diameter

3 dried ivy leaves

Pruning shears

Scissors

Green floral tape

3 pieces of medium-gauge floral wire, 4 inches long

6-inch-diameter paper doily cuff

Hot-glue gun and glue sticks

Wire cutters

18 inches of wide red satin ribbon

3 yards of narrow red satin ribbon

## WHAT YOU DO

1 Arrange the oregano stems in five bunches, the tansy in five bunches, and the pennyroyal in five bunches.

2 Combine the oregano, tansy, and pennyroyal bunches to make three larger bunches, hot-gluing the hydrangea pieces to each one. Using the pruning shears, cut the stems of each bunch at an angle to reduce their thickness.

3 To strengthen the stems, use the floral tape to attach a 4-inch length of floral wire to the base of each bunch.

4 Tape two of the bunches together. Then tape the third bunch to the other two.

5 Slip the taped stems through the hole in the doily cuff. Add some hot glue to the inside face of the doily just around the edge of the hole, and press the doily gently against the base of the bouquet.

6 Using the wire cutters, cut the stems and the wires off at the desired length. Then use the wide ribbon to wrap the stems from the base of the doily all the way to the bottom, hot-gluing the ribbon as you wrap it in place.

7 Hot-glue the zinnias throughout the bouquet, placing the largest toward the center.

8 Hot-glue the ivy leaves throughout the bouquet, varying their angles to add visual interest.

9 Cut the narrow ribbon into two equal lengths. Place the lengths side by side and make an eight-loop bow with four streamers (see "Bows" on page 46). Cut the streamers to the desired lengths and hot-glue the bow between the doily and the bouquet.

# TWIGS

Furniture and decorative items made from branches and twigs are called "rustic," and the best designers in this field are those who can visualize the finished piece while it's still part of a living tree. You can use many different types of wood for rustic craft projects; birch, dogwood, hemlock, silver maple, sycamore, and willow are particularly suitable. Avoid any kind of pine because the sap tends to run after the wood has been cut, making the wood sticky. Experiment with different woods to learn the properties of each type—some will be sturdy while others will be more flexible. But remember, don't cut trees that are endangered species.

Although you can cut wood all year long, the best time of year is winter or late fall when the sap is down. Unless your project calls for removing the bark, leave it on. If you find a tree or branch on the ground, examine it to see if it's rotten; if it crushes or breaks easily, leave it. When you find wood you like, cut it with a saw or pruning shears and trim off any parts you don't want. Cut the branches as long as possible since you can always cut them into smaller pieces later.

For most craft applications, you'll want to work with dry wood. Wood shrinks as it dries and may warp, so it's useful to see what form the dry wood takes before you use it. The rule of thumb is that wood air-dries at a rate of 1 inch in diameter a year. This means that even a small twig the thickness of a pencil will take a few months to dry completely. You can use fresh-cut wood if you nail it together and don't mind the bends and twists that will develop as the wood dries. When storing your wood, remember to store it in a cool, dry place. (For additional information on how to form twig bases, see "Making a Twig Base" on page 18.)

*If you need an unusual backdrop for your favorite dried flowers, consider this simple twig trellis.*

# Twig Trellis

## WHAT YOU NEED

12 green, straight twigs: six 13 inches long, four 4 inches long, two 12 inches long, and all ¾ inch in diameter

3 lengths of honeysuckle or other thin vine, 24 inches long

Cornhusk scraps

4 sprigs of dried German statice dyed pink, 3 inches long

4 dried pink roses

1-inch-long common nails

Hammer

Clear acrylic varnish

Paintbrush

4 yards of cotton ribbon, ½ inch wide

Scissors

Spool of thin-gauge floral wire

Hat pin

Hot-glue gun and glue sticks

## WHAT YOU DO

1 Place the six 13-inch-long twigs vertically on your work surface. With the ends lined up and all the twigs touching side-to-side, sandwich them between two of the 4-inch-long twigs placed horizontally across and about 1½ inches from the bottom of the six 13-inch-long twigs. Starting in the middle of the top 4-inch-long twig, nail through that twig, into one of the 13-inch-long twigs, and through the 4-inch-long twig on the bottom. Repeat this process with each of the six 13-inch-long twigs. Then sandwich the six 13-inch-long twigs between two more 4-inch-long twigs, four inches up from the other set of horizontal twigs, and nail them together in the same way.

2 Sandwich the top end of the six 13-inch-long twigs between the two 12-inch-long twigs in the same manner as in Step 1. Starting on one side, bend a vertical twig so it curves gently out to one side, and nail through the "twig sandwich" as in Step 1. As you fasten each of the other five twigs, fan each out and gently bend the horizontal twigs into an arch.

3 Weave the three lengths of honeysuckle or other thin vine around and through the twig frame. Paint the entire trellis with the clear acrylic varnish and allow it to dry for one to two hours.

4 Make a multiple-loop bow with the cotton ribbon (see "Bows" on page 46). Using a piece of the thin-gauge floral wire, attach the bow to the front of the trellis between the two 4-inch-long twigs.

5 Shred the cornhusk scraps by running the hat pin all the way through them. Make two cornhusk "bouquets" by wrapping a piece of the thin-gauge floral wire around each of the two bundles of shredded husks, close to one end. Then trim the ends of the husks below the wire. Hot-glue the cornhusk bouquets to the bow, and hot-glue the German statice and the four roses to the center of the bow.

*Fill the completed basket with an arrangement of dried flowers and foliage, or line it with a pretty piece of fabric and use it as a gift container.*

# Twig Basket

## WHAT YOU NEED

8 dried twigs, 7½ inches long
and ½ inch in diameter

12 dried twigs, 10 inches long
and ¾ inch in diameter

1 flexible green twig, 24 inches long
and ¾ inch wide

Tack hammer

Small finishing nails

Sharp knife

1 to 2 feet of any kind of vine

## WHAT YOU DO

*1* To make the base of the basket, place four of the 7½-inch-long twigs between two of the 10-inch-long twigs, spacing each one as shown in Figure 1. Then use the tack hammer to drive the finishing nails through the rounded sides of the longer twigs and into the ends of the shorter ones, as shown in the photograph below. Exact measurements are not critical in this project, but you will want to leave space for two additional 7½-inch-long twigs, one at each end of the base; these will be added in Step 3.

*2* To assemble the sides, first study Figure 2. Note that the sides are constructed by stacking the 10-inch-long twigs log-cabin style and nailing them together, one by one. Space the twigs to create an interior that is about 7½ inches square. Stack the twigs to overlap each other by about ½ inch, nailing each twig to the one below it. After the basket sides are assembled, place one 7½-inch-long twig between each of the 10-inch-long twigs that form the top layer of the basket's sides. Nail the 7½-inch-long twigs to the 10-inch-long twigs underneath as shown in the photograph below.

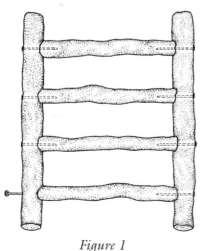

*Figure 1*

*Figure 2*

*3* Turn the assembled sides upside down and place the base on top. Nail the base to the twigs underneath it and, for extra support, add the remaining two 7½-inch-long twigs at either end, nailing them in place, as shown in the photograph below.

*4* Using a sharp knife, whittle each end of the 24-inch-long flexible green twig to flatten the inner surfaces so that it will rest evenly against the sides of the basket. Then bend and position the handle on the basket. Drive finishing nails through each end of the handle and into the twigs forming the sides of the basket. The handle may twist somewhat as it dries. Wrap strands of vine around the corners of the basket and where the handle is attached.

# Root & Flower Wreath

## WHAT YOU NEED

6 of last year's scented geranium roots or other interesting roots found during spring cleanup, in various sizes

12 × 15-inch oval grapevine base

2 pieces of sheet moss, 12 inches square

1 small handful of any kind of feathery lichen

60 miscellaneous dried flower heads, including hydrangea, strawflower, and globe amaranth

10 dried green leaves, any kind

1 interesting cone or pod

Pruning shears

Spool of medium-gauge floral wire

Wire cutters

Hot-glue gun and glue sticks

Scissors

## WHAT YOU DO

*1* Shake off any dirt still attached to the roots. (If the roots are heavily covered with dirt, you may want to rinse them in water.) Using the pruning shears, trim them until there is a little of the main stem and 5 to 6 inches of root remaining. Cover half of the grapevine base with the roots, attaching them with pieces of the medium-gauge floral wire, starting with the largest root at the top and the smallest on the sides. Overlap and intertwine the roots as you wire them to the base. To secure the roots, apply hot glue between the wires and the base. It will take two or three generous applications of hot glue to hold the bulkiest roots in place.

*2* Using the scissors, cut the sheet moss into 20 pieces, each 2 inches square. Hot-glue the pieces to the base in a random pattern, placing most over the bottom half of the base and some pieces between the roots. Glue the lichen in the same manner, but place most of it on the inner rim for maximum effect.

*3* Break the hydrangea into small blooms. Using hot glue, attach the hydrangea and remaining flower heads and leaves to the wreath in a pleasing arrangement, gluing most of the flowers onto the bottom half. Don't overdo it by covering too many of the root shapes. Hot-glue the cone or pod to the top section of the wreath, slightly off-center.

*Gnarled roots and delicate flowers are paired in this unusual and dazzling wreath.*

# Wild Wreath

## WHAT YOU NEED

8 to 10 lengths of kudzu, 6 feet long
(If kudzu is not available, substitute
wisteria or grapevine.)

Assorted grasses in various lengths,
6 to 15 inches long

6 rose hips, with stems 6 inches long

Several dried insects (optional)

Hot-glue gun and glue sticks

## WHAT YOU DO

*1* Remove all of the leaves from the
kudzu vine. Using one vine length,
form a circle 14 inches in diameter, twisting the lead end around the rest of the
vine to hold the circle shape. Wind the rest
of the length of the vine around the circle.
Add the other lengths of kudzu by twisting
and intertwining them until the base is the
thickness you want (see "Making a Vine
Wreath Base" on page 18).

*2* Lay all of the grasses in groups in
front of you so you can choose from
their various textures and colors. The
kinds of grasses you will find will depend
on where you live. Some common varieties include timothy, redtop, foxtail,
rough bristle, feather, reed canary
(*Phalaris arundinacea*), switch, sudan,
reed, and bottlebrush.

*3* Start with the bulkiest grasses and
hot-glue them evenly all around the
wreath in one direction; put only a small
dab of hot glue on the grass and be careful not to burn your fingers when you
press the grass onto the base.

*A swirl arrangement, like the wind
blowing through a field, is perfectly
suited to wild materials.*

*4* Fashion clusters with all the other
grasses and the rose hips. Tuck and
hot-glue the clusters around the wreath in
the same direction as the first layer of the
grass. You want to have grasses at different
heights and on different visual planes so
that the wreath has movement and full-
ness. Fill in wherever you see gaps by hot-
gluing small tufts of the grasses to the
base. To complete the wild effect, you can
hot-glue dried insects to the wreath.